Data Driven Sales Ops

The Sales Operations Manager's Guide to
Driving Action from Insight

Jeff Nguyen

Contents

Introduction   IV

1. Understanding Your Data   1

2. Identifying Key Metrics and KPIs   9

3. From Data to Insights   17

4. Foundations of Data Visualization   27

5. The Impact of Data-Driven Stories   43

6. How to Build a Data-Driven Story   59

7. Communicating Insights Through Data-Driven Story-   73
   telling

8. Aligning Data Visualization with Business Goals   80

9. Data-Driven Decision-Making   93

10. Applications of Data Stories in Sales Operations   107

11. Conclusion   121

Introduction

Whether you're a sales leader, operations professional, or team member looking to maximize revenue. Data and insights are playing an increasingly important role in guiding commercial success, yet information alone does little without meaningful context and application. This is where data storytelling comes in as a core sales operations capability.

At its core, data-driven storytelling entails combining analytical expertise with business acumen, customer understanding, and process insights to transform raw metrics into compelling narratives. It melds the science of statistical analysis with the art of resonating communication tailored to driving outcomes.

On the technical side, proficient data storytellers adeptly manipulate and analyze volumes of data from channels like CRM and marketing automation platforms, blended with external market inputs. Leveraging latest visualization and business intelligence technologies, they synthesize complex datasets into clear, focused stories spotlighting crucial performance patterns, gaps and opportunities - rather than just passively reporting scattered statistics in silos.

But masterful storytelling requires more than just analytical skills. Strong interpersonal abilities prove equally key for communicating contextualized insights effectively to influence the behaviors of various commercial teams. Sales operations storytelling specialists work closely with field leaders, account managers, and frontline representatives to intimately comprehend overlapping as well as distinct objectives, challenges and pain points faced.

Armed with this multidimensional understanding, data storytellers carefully select and frame the most relevant metrics to craft resonating narratives customized to each specific audience and scenario. For example, they create guidance helping representatives prioritize prospecting outreach based on proven customer profile indicators or inform executives seeking to optimize sales territory structures and resource allocation plans based on quantitatively validated success drivers.

Applied thoughtfully, data-driven storytelling allows sales operations leaders to directly impact revenue results in profoundly new ways not possible through traditional reporting. By distilling endless streams of complex data points into simplified, memorable narratives embedded with key discoveries, data storytellers provide field sellers with crisp, actionable inputs to guide daily decisions. This prescriptive guidance helps customer-facing teams maximize the relevance of every interaction while shortening sales cycles through optimized pitches rooted in empirical evidence.

Alongside field teams, storytelling helps sales operations better meet the needs of executives as well by validating proposed strategies with hard, verifiable data - building consensus across departments essential for unified action. For example, analytics quantifying the revenue expansion potential across customer segments helps justify proposed new vertical targets to enter. Benchmarking diagnostics proving inferior win rates for net new logos versus existing accounts compels leadership commitment to consolidating expansion. These analytical narratives ground recommendations in irrefutable realities, overcoming doubts founded on intuition rather than facts.

Through consistent, scalable data narrative framing applied across scenarios, sales operations can gain unprecedented visibility into emerging performance patterns and shifts in markets, competitive forces and customer behaviors. With expanding volumes of CRM, external and operational signals streaming continuously, specialist storytellers fulfill an indispensable role curating the most crucial discoveries while filtering less valuable information overload. Applying principles like change analysis and drill-down diagnostics, they continually analyze current and historical data to accurately identify highly effective commercial movements that boost deal conversion. This empirical validation then informs corresponding improvements across methodologies, messaging content, and platform tools to optimize selling based on the latest situational realities.

Furthermore, with insights exposing specific skill deficiencies impeding field team development, data-driven storytelling paves the path for sales operations to pinpoint precise training interventions needed at scale to nurture seller success executing prescribed strategies. For example, analytics may reveal new mobile conversational selling tools require reinforcing for adoption before corresponding to positive trends in sales velocity and win rates. Once addressed through focused coaching, deploying updated tactics bears fruit. In these ways, fact-based storytelling reinforcement cycles organically propagate operational excellence over time.

With immense potential benefits but significant analytical rigor and communication expertise needed, many leading enterprises now choose to formally establish data-driven storytelling as a dedicated sales operations specialty function. Locating this strategic capability directly within sales operations units allows maximal alignment to core revenue generation priorities, more autonomy over foundational data inputs and governance policies, and direct collaborative accessibility for both sales executives and customer-facing professionals.

When deeply embedded alongside traditional enablement, analytics and process functions, data storytelling not only unlocks profound new revenue and customer insights - it also elevates complexity management. With data volumes across systems continuing to rise exponentially amidst disruption, masterful narrative development proves ever crucial for curating only the most valid and impactful kernels of insight needed from a sea of indicators. This eliminaties less predictive vanity or siloed metrics, insightful framing concentrates collective attention exclusively on empirically verified strategic and tactical sales drivers which in turn gives sales a renewed clarity of direction. Executed with nuance and care for audiences through research-backed communications principles, resonating data is conevrted into condensed stories that then sticks in memories while motivating targeted actions aligned to growth outcomes.

Savvy enterprises increasingly recognize data-driven storytelling capabilities as pivotal in cementing competitive advantage. This is especially so within disrupted commercial environments flooded with exponentially growing information. Designing mature storytelling strategies delivers compounding returns over the long-run through continuous optimization and alignment of selling motions, marketing campaigns, capability development and operational upgrades based wholly on data revealing customer needs.

When new buyer behaviors or disruptive technologies require sales transformations, insightful data narratives guide change management and vital reskilling. This is done by equipping stakeholders at all levels with tangible evidence explaining why adjustments remain essential to sustaining relevance. Also, grounding recommendations in verifiable proof accelerates acceptance.

As consultative, insight-based selling fast becomes more and more important for resonance amid market complexity, sustained investments in enterprise-class data narrative specialization ensure sales units fully activate informational resources as differentiators driving peak team performance. Simply put, any modern sales organization seeking pole position in propelling consistent revenue and customer growth should prioritize cultivating robust data storytelling muscles across its operational toolkit.

To wrap up, data-driven storytelling blends statistical analysis, impactful visualization and profound empathy for diverse audiences to transform scattered data points into resonant narratives that motivate revenue growth behaviors across organizations. Masterful context-aware story framing allows sales operations to influence critical decisions at scale, optimize commercial methodologies empirically for efficiency and direct capability advancement in response to fluid situational realities.

While exponential information growth generates complexity risks, dedicated data narrative builders mitigate chaos. Condensing overwhelming signals into memorable simplified stories proves pivotal in extracting essential insights needed from swelling data repositories by various sales stakeholders seeking custom answers for their unique questions. When strategically embedded across sales technology stacks and processes through specialized storyteller roles, insights activation unlocks immense latent potential within data assets remaining largely untapped otherwise.

I hope this guide provides you with enhanced clarity on how data storytelling can profoundly strengthen sales operations' strategic influence and revenue impact. Whether you decide to hire dedicated specialists or cross-skill current analysts with communications training, huge opportunities exist to derive exponential new value from information using context-aware narrative techniques. Prioritizing organizational data storytelling fluency paves a clear pathway to commercial leadership within a marketplace where making sense of complexity counts most.

Chapter 1
Understanding Your Data

S ales analytics is the process of collecting and analyzing data about the sales team, the customers, and the market in order to improve the sales process.

The importance and influence of sales analytics is growing across nearly every industry. One of the main factors driving this trend is that sales processes are more complex than they have ever been before, making it necessary to find ways to simplify and streamline them. The best way to do this is to make data-driven decisions that directly impact your sales team and its results. However, there are two key challenges facing organizations:

1. **Data quality assurance:** The volume of data collected is increasing at an exponential rate. Salespeople have access to more information than ever before through resources such as social media and customer relationship management (CRM) software; however, sales managers must first determine how much of this information is valuable for their purposes. Also, you have to ensure that the data you collect is accurate. You can't manage what you don't measure, and it's important to make sure that the metrics you choose are

relevant for your organization.

2. **Finding Insights from data:** The present tools are not fully capable of transforming this massive amount of data into helpful insights. Even if a company had a perfect view of its customers' needs and wants, it would still need to put this information into practice.

But one way to successfully manage data flow is to strategically choose the appropriate inputs for your needs. You should know what you want to achieve with your data, and then choose the best tools that can help you achieve those goals. The more specific you are in defining what you want to measure and how you want to measure it, the easier it will be to find a solution.

Profile the Data Source

Data profiling is the practice of studying, analyzing, reviewing, and summarizing data sets in order to get insight on data quality. Data quality is a metric that assesses the state of data based on variables such as correctness, completeness, consistency, reliability, and accessibility.

In order to obtain a clear picture of the overall data set, it must be broken down into components that can be individually analyzed. For example, if you have a dataset that contains marketing campaign data from the last five years, you can break down the dataset by year and then by quarter to examine year-over-year growth or decline of different marketing channels for each quarter. This allows for targeted analysis of data instead of looking at the whole picture at once. Not only does it make it much easier to identify patterns within the data set; it also makes it easier to spot patterns in outliers and determine whether they are anomalies or valid trends.

Data profiling can also be used to help an organization determine if their data infrastructure is sufficient to contain and analyze new types of data being collected. In addition to identifying trends in structured data like spreadsheets and databases, organizations should also examine unstructured data like reports and emails.

The first step of data profiling is gathering one or multiple data sources and the associated metadata for analysis. The metadata provides information on the origin of the source and its structure. This stage also allows you to determine whether there are any data quality issues that need to be addressed, before proceeding with actual analysis.

The next step is data preparation. This is the process of organizing, cleaning and transforming data. This step is necessary to ensure that the data can be used in a meaningful way. It involves eliminating duplicate records, correcting errors, and creating relationships between different datasets. The goal is to organize the information into a clean format that can be easily analyzed and manipulated.

In the world of business intelligence, data profiling is one of the most important processes to conduct before embarking on an analytics project to ensure that the data set is clean and accurate. This process will allow you to identify key attributes and measures to use as well as potential measurements for assessing the quality of the data.

Control the Data

Data control is an important part of the analytics process, but a lot of companies tend to overlook it. Whether they don't realize they should be doing it or they don't have a plan in place, the result is still the same: they don't have access to the information they need to make decisions and improve their business.

Data control is management oversight of information policies for an organization's information. Unlike data quality, which focuses on fixing problems, data control is observing and reporting on how processes are working and managing issues. Functions include inspection, validation, notification, documentation, issue reporting, and issue tracking.

The focus, for sales ops, is to ensure completeness and consistency. This ensures inputs like addresses, emails, phone numbers, and client names are kept in a uniform format and comply with local conventions. For example, zip codes and phone numbers contain the correct number of digits.

Data control is important because it helps organizations ensure that:

- Data is properly handled and used.

- Information is accurate, complete, and available when needed.

- Standards and procedures are followed.

There are additional facets to data control such as ensuring the right users have access to the right information, and blocking or limiting access as necessary. Data security is a shared responsibility, although not the focus of our discussion here.

Best Practices for Data Profiling & Control

The importance of data profiling and control is often overlooked in favor of more interesting and complex data integration tasks. In fact, poor quality data can lead to lost customers, increase costs and undermine the effectiveness of business processes. It can also cause frustration for employees who have to manually clean up errors and inconsistencies that are found in the data.

In order to prevent these problems, a company must have a process that ensures that their customer data is complete and accurate. This process should include:

- Correct highly visible and often used data, such as addresses and emails. Remove any duplicate information. Check the data for accuracy and consistency by comparing the database with other records.

- Install filters at all client interface points, particularly the Web. These filters serve as a first line of defense against bad data. They prevent invalid, incomplete or inconsistent data from getting into the system in the first place. This approach is more efficient than trying to clean up after the fact, because it prevents problems before they occur.

- Use validation rules to notify users when data records are missing or do not meet data quality criteria. These rules can be applied during data entry or as an additional step when a user saves a record. Validation rules are also useful for detecting duplicates and other problems in your database. For example, if you have two records with the same primary key value, then one of the records is likely invalid.

- Provide automated exception reports/dashboards to management. This is an important step, because it will help reduce the amount of manual work needed to find and fix data quality problems. The report should also indicate which records have been reviewed by users and approved for entry into your database.

A comprehensive Customer Data Integration solution contains the following components: connection, grouping, customer recognition, and cleanliness.

Integrate the Data

In order to create a 360° view of your customers and their purchase history, you must combine your order entry and fulfillment tools with your CRM to get a comprehensive view of your customers. A good way to start is to examine your applications to see which one will be the master record during the synchronization procedure. The master record is the main customer information in the system that all other related applications will use during synchronization. This allows you to have one unique customer identifier that can be used throughout your organization.

Not only does the integration allow you to track their interactions with the sales team, it also allows you to track their interactions with the support team, the billing department and anyone else who inter-acts with them. This allows you to not only provide better customer service but also build a deeper relationship with your customers.

The integration between systems also allows you to see how well your sales team is performing. You can see who is making their quota, who isn't and what they need to do differently. This will allow you to make better hiring decisions in the future as well as improve the quality of your sales force.

Validate your Data

For firms that rely on sales analytics, the temptation to trust in tech-nology can be strong. Data cleansing, validation, and integration are all time-consuming. However, while technology has made some strides in recent years, it cannot be relied upon solely.

Utilizing the capabilities of your CRM system is one way to be sure that you're taking advantage of all the data it has to offer and that you're getting the most from it. Having a solid understanding of your sales data will help you discover trends, patterns, and opportunities that might otherwise be missed. It can also help you identify problems within your process or product offering that need addressing. You should never underestimate the value of having a human eye on the data; even if there are some things that technology cannot do well (yet).

Technology tools can aid your efforts, but they cannot replace vigilance of your business processes. You'll also want to make sure that you're supplementing these technological capabilities by being careful about your data's quality, sound processes for ensuring accurate and reliable results throughout the life cycle, and solutions from third-party providers and professional services organizations. This will help you to avoid the pitfalls that come with relying on a single tool or technology provider. You need to be able to keep your eyes open, so to speak, and think critically about how you can use these tools effectively in order to achieve your goals.

It's also important to keep in mind that the data that you're collecting is not just a "nice-to-have." It's a critical component of your business operations, which means that there are many reasons why you'll want to validate it regularly. The best way to do this is with a data audit or data quality assessment.

This is a process where you evaluate your data and determine whether it's accurate, complete and reliable. This means profiling it and checking your controls regularly. It's also important to remember that data quality is not something you can achieve once and then forget about. It's an ongoing process, which means that you'll want to continually be evaluating your data for accuracy and completeness. This is especially true if you're using AI tools in your sales and marketing efforts, since these tools rely on accurate data sets in order to work effectively.

Key Takeaways

- Profile your data sources to analyze quality and suitability for your needs before starting analytics. Break the data into components for targeted insights.

- Implement data controls like validation rules and automated monitoring to ensure completeness, accuracy, and consistency. This saves time versus fixing issues later.

- Prioritize highly visible data elements like names, emails, addresses. Use filters to catch bad data at entry points.

- Create a master customer record during system integration to enable a single source of truth across sales, support, billing etc.

- Supplement analytics software by manually verifying quality. Regularly audit with statistical checks and human review.

- Treat data as a critical business asset. Continually monitor completeness and accuracy, especially when using AI tools.

Chapter 2
Identifying Key Metrics and KPIs

A s a sales operations professional, you play a crucial role in identifying and selecting the key performance indicators (KPIs) used to gauge success. However, not all data offers equal value. The art entails pinpointing metrics aligned to strategic objectives that provide practical, actionable insights into what is working, what is not, and where improvements may lie. This discussion focuses on the components of effective KPI selection, emphasizing relevance, measurability, and strategic alignment.

Set Precise, Aligned Measures of Success

Organizations must set precise measures aligned to business objectives to gauge sales performance. While specific metrics will differ across companies, sales operations should concentrate on a few essential variables tied to strategic goals. For example, use revenue growth rate targets to track progress towards profitability aims or customer retention rate goals to monitor customer experience efforts. The emphasis falls on defining quantifiable KPIs that offer decisive inputs into what success looks like.

KPIs Should be Specific, Measurable, and Time-Bound

When reviewing past performance to shape future strategies, begin by precisely defining key performance indicators. KPIs should be specific and measurable. For instance, "grow revenue by 15% over the next year" sets a clear, quantitative aim easy to track. Vague ambitions like "grow our business" lack the clarity required to effectively assess outcomes. Additionally, incorporate timebound elements aligned to business planning cycles. Estalishing quarterly or annual aims enables bite-sized progress monitoring.

Categorize KPIs by Performance, Efficiency, and Effectiveness

The most crucial KPIs for sales operations generally fall under performance, efficiency, or effectiveness categories. Sales performance tracks revenue expansion outcomes against goals. For example, compare actual quarterly sales results versus quarterly budgets to identify over or underperformance. Meanwhile, sales efficiency KPIs reveal costs associated with revenue generation. Assess expenses from sales activities against won deals to expose resource intensive areas needing optimization. Lastly, blend performance and efficiency KPIs to calculate sales effectiveness, determining if investments pay off. If a sales team falls short of revenue goals despite heavy time investments, effectiveness diminishes.

Uncover Why: The Power of Diagnostic Metrics

While KPI dashboards spotlight what outcomes transpired, diagnostic metrics reveal why by spotlighting inputs driving the results. For example, examine lead follow-up, call connect, and deal close rates to expose weaknesses impeding revenue performance. Low follow-up rates signal issues engaging new prospects. High call connect but low close rates suggest opportunities getting wasted. Comparing diagnostic indicators across teams or regions quickly highlights where and sometimes why results vary.

The most important KPIs for sales operations fall into two categories: performance and efficiency.

Sales Performance Metrics

Sales performance analytics can provide a wealth of information about the sales team's performance and progress. Newer CRMs feature metrics such as Forecast Accuracy and Pipeline Value help to answer a lot of questions that have traditionally been tough to pin down, such as "How well are my people performing, and how is this affecting the pipeline?" or "How much money can we expect to make?" Here's a quick rundown of some of the most valuable benefits that sales analytics bring to the table.

Sales quota achievement rate: The percentage of sellers who have completely hit their quota during a set time period. It's an excellent way to keep track of how hard your team is working and just how much they're earning for the company. It also shows you if there are any key leads that are going cold—and why.

Win rate: This is an indicator of how good your salespeople are at closing deals. It also highlights which are your top performers—you can see who should be emulated by other sellers, and who needs some training or support in order to improve their win rates.

Deal size: The average value of deal sizes that sellers manage at any time. This is great for forecasting the overall value of your pipeline, but it can also highlight certain gaps in your sales team's ability to get large deals closed.

Pipeline Value: The estimated value of the pipeline in a set time in each stage of the sales process. It shows how much revenue you could expect to make if all deals currently in the pipeline are closed. This is an important metric because it can highlight any issues with your sales team's ability to close deals, such as low win rates or slow deal velocity.

Forecast Accuracy: The error rates of predicted forecasts versus actual results can indicate how well the sales team is forecasting revenue. If your forecasts are consistently inaccurate, this could mean that your sales team doesn't have a good understanding of how to estimate deals or that there's a problem with their process.

It's important to keep in mind that these metrics will change over time as you hire more people, train them up and have them focus on different types of deals. But they're a good way to see how well your sales team is performing overall—and they can help you identify what needs improving so that you can start earning more revenue.

Sales Efficiency Metrics

Sales efficiency analytics is a valuable tool for sales executives and managers to use in order to effectively assess the performance of their sales teams. By focusing on the metrics that have the most impact on revenue and performance, sales executives can determine which areas of the sales process need improvement, and how to go about changing them.

Length of Sales Cycle: The average amount of time it takes for sellers to close deals is one of the more important metrics tracked by sales analytics; this data can be used to predict how long it will take to close future deals based on historical data, and help set target dates for deals that need certain timelines for completion. This information also helps sales executives determine what types of deals are most profitable for their company, as well as whether there are specific team members who are more effective at closing certain types of deals than others.

Selling Time: The actual time sellers are "in the field" selling compared to other duties like meetings, training, and administrative tasks is another common metric tracked by sales executives. The ratio of selling time to non-selling time can be used to determine whether the sales team is being productive in their day-to-day activities, as well as whether they are spending too much time on administrative tasks such as paperwork and reporting.

Lead Response Time: The time it takes leads to positively respond to pitches or calls to action is another common metric tracked by sales executives. Lead response time can be used to determine if the sales team is spending too much or too little time on each lead and whether they are closing deals at a desirable rate.

Prospect Meetings: The number of meetings each seller sets up in a set amount of time compared to the prospecting activity for that seller is another good metric to track. This can help you see if your staff is doing an adequate amount of selling or if they need more training on how to effectively move deals forward with customers.

Pipeline Efficiency: How effectively sellers manage their individual pipelines is another important metric to track. You can use this information to determine if your salespeople are properly prioritizing opportunities and managing their time effectively.

Once your sales metrics are defined, you should regularly review them in order to optimize your strategies. This is especially relevant for sales operations teams, as they have access to the systems of record that contain the majority of this data. Create useful dashboards with business intelligence and CRM products so you can refer to them when issuing strategy throughout each quarter.

In order to stay on top of your sales metrics, you should have a monthly reporting cycle. This will allow you to identify trends in your data and make adjustments based on the information you find. You can also set up a dashboard that includes the most critical metrics so that everyone in your organization knows what they should be focusing on at any given time.

This will allow you to quickly identify which tactics are performing well and which ones could use some optimization. The most important thing to remember when you're setting up your metrics is that they should be actionable. You want to be able to use the data in order to make decisions about what changes need to be made, but it doesn't have much value if you can't do anything with it.

Align KPIs to Business Goals

Selecting the right key performance indicators (KPIs) provides the foundation for aligning data analytics to business objectives. The process entails pinpointing precise, quantified metrics offering decisive visibility into progress made towards top-level goals. This discussion spotlights best practices to consider when assessing and choosing measurement indicators for sales operations.

Assess Relevance to Sales Operations Priorities

Not all metrics offer equal utility. Focus first on evaluating potential KPIs based on relevance to current sales operations priorities and challenges. For example, indicators tracking customer churn rates, sales cycle times or contract values provide direct, tangible inputs into metrics sales managers care about most. The emphasis falls on isolating measures that sharply illuminate performance levels on the outcomes most crucial for short and long-term success.

Tightly Align KPIs to Business Strategies

Ensure rigorous alignment between selected key indicators and overarching organizational strategies. For example, Firm X wants to improve customer retention and loyalty amidst rising competition. In support, sales operations leaders establish customer churn rate and net promoter score KPIs to spotlight progress towards this strategic priority. Tight strategic alignment provides context and prevents tracking measures solely because data exists to produce them.

Quantifiable KPIs Enable Decisive Insights

Choose indicators offering clear quantitative outputs. Metrics directly fueling performance assessment through numerical outputs provide tangibility often lacking in qualitative measures prone to interpretation differences. Sales managers likely care more about weekly sales conversion rates, average deal sizes, and aging sales funnel indicators than subjective satisfaction scores. Quantifiable KPIs lend decisive clarity.

Consider Data Availability Constraints

Account for data availability constraints when selecting key performance indicators. The data, human resources, financials and technologies required to accurately measure and consistently produce a metric at necessary cadences should align to current analytics capabilities. There is no benefit in tracking indicators that teams lack the infrastructure scale to reliably support.

Establish Benchmarking to Contextualize Performance

Leverage benchmarking to provide context around sales operations performance results, which amplifies insights versus assessing indicators in isolation. For example, record current average sales cycle durations, than establish benchmarks based on historical performance or industry standards to quantify status as below average, average or above average. This instantly spotlights over or underperformance.

The practices above help build relevance, alignment and contextualization into the metrics at the core of data-driven monitoring and decision making.

Key Takeaways

- Set precise, quantifiable measures of success aligned to strategic business goals to enable decisive insights into performance.

- Categorize metrics by performance, efficiency and effectiveness to isolate crucial outcome and process indicators.

- Use diagnostic metrics to uncover why results occurred by exposing input drivers behind outcomes.

- Regularly review core sales metrics like quota achievement, win rate and pipeline value to spotlight performance.

- Assess efficiency metrics like sales cycle length and prospect meetings to find process weak points.

- Ensure tight alignment between KPI selection and overarching organizational priorities and strategies.

- Consider data availability constraints and benchmarking when choosing indicators to provide context.

Chapter 3
From Data to Insights

As a sales operations professional, you likely have access to extensive data on customers, products, and sales performance. However, simply collecting data does little good on its own. To drive real value, you need to be able to convert raw information into strategic insights that guide impactful decisions and demonstrably improve results. In this piece, I'll spotlight key principles to help you transform disconnected data inputs into decisive, actionable intelligence.

Rather than only reporting sporadic basic observations using spreadsheets, focus on performing robust analysis to uncover patterns and insights within your company's data. Identify relationships between factors that influence sales, such as regional differences, customer segments, product mixes, and more. Look for performance trends over time. And determine where there may be gaps or opportunities for improvement. Use advanced analytics tools and statistical models as appropriate to facilitate revealing vital insights.

The most critical step comes next - activating the intelligence by tying insights directly to strategy, planning and execution. Share findings across departments and ensure they directly inform everything from pricing decisions to sales training priorities. Continually track performance against data-driven plans to quantify the tangible impact over time.

With a comprehensive analytics strategy that converts granular data into strategic insights, and tight alignment to strategy and operations, sales ops can elevate from passive reporting to actively driving gains. By following these principles, you'll be enabled to unlock more value from your data.

Evolve From Reporting Observations to Uncovering Patterns

A foundational data analytics capability entails looking beyond isolated datapoints to uncover the crucial performance patterns, trends and relationships connecting them. For example, rather than merely reporting weekly revenue results, employ historical comparisons to quantify growth trajectories. Examine regional or product line contributions to highlight areas over or underperforming against expectations. Uncovering connections and variability empowers projecting future outcomes based on validated assumptions.

Analytics Fuel Predictions Grounded in Facts

Prediction represents the ultimate stage of leveraging data effectively. Reporting what happened provides hindsight. Pattern analysis delivers insight into what is happening. Forecasting offers visibility into what will likely happen next. For example, product sales data revealing customer retention challenges can support prediction models estimating future churn risks. This enables preemptive mitigations to prevent losses. However, predictions require sufficient historical inputs to establish legitimate statistical models rather than guesses.

Actionable Intelligence Informs Strategies, Decisions

The measure of effective data analysis involves the ability to drive better strategies and decisions through actionable insights. If examination of sales pipeline stages exposes 70% of deals stalling at proposal approvals, sales operations can build compressed approval playbooks to increase win rates. When product returns spike, analytics linking complaints to technical issues inform corrective quality initiatives. Across functions, data holds negligible value absent integration into choices that measurably move revenue, efficiency or experience needles.

Centralize Analytics with Flexible Platforms

Achieving enterprise-wide utilization requires transitioning from makeshift spreadsheet analyses. Centralized, cloud-based analytics platforms enable secure access to integrated, governed datasets that specialists can model to meet varied functional needs. For example, align sales, marketing and support teams around core KPI dashboards, deliver self-service insights to managers, and fuel advanced analytics for executives – all from unified, trusted information. Removing data siloes powers collaboration.

Realizing value from burgeoning information requires evolution from reporting observations to enabling action through integrated analytics. Deriving decisions and strategies from centralized, governed data platforms helps sales operations progress across the maturity spectrum – from fragmented insights to propelling competitive advantages through prediction capabilities grounded in operational realities.

What Are Data Insights?

Many organizations excel at gathering data yet struggle to derive value from the accumulating volumes they store. Creating impact requires evolving raw datasets into insights that influence better strategies, decisions and outcomes. Data insights should:

1. Uncover Patterns

2. Shift Perspectives

3. Inform Decisions

Progress From Observing Data to Uncovering Patterns

Raw data encompasses factual inputs like sales transaction records. Analytics involves examining datasets to expose influential patterns, trends and connections amidst the numbers. For example, rather than simply tallying weekly revenue, compare results against prior years. Seek variances pointing to changes in customer behaviors, seasonal impacts or broader economic shifts. The goal is identifying patterns to supplement facts with crucial context that explains what is occurring.

Insights Shift Perspectives to Compel Action

Data insights build upon pattern analysis to deliver breakthroughs that fundamentally shift mindsets and compel actions. Psychologist Gary Klein defines insights as "a shift in the way we understand things." The B2C retailer discovering a subset of international resellers amidst customer data experienced this very revelation, unlocking cascade of new considerations around product, pricing and global expansion opportunities now visible.

Insights are only as valuable as the actions they provoke. Observations should inform decisions that drive desired outcomes, whether revenue gains, cost savings or experience improvements. If uncovered patterns do not culminate in measurable strategic impacts, analyzing data delivers minimal return on investment, no matter how intriguing the interim discoveries.

Centralize and Share Insights to Inform Decisions

Transitioning from fragmented reporting to centralized analytics platforms marks a pivotal step in amplifying data value. Consolidating customer information and sales records from across systems exposes multifaceted insights impossible to discern in information silos.

Further, secure cloud platforms enable publishing findings directly to decision-makers, ensuring insights shape choices.

For example, alerts highlighting unusual spikes in product returns can prompt executives to pause shipments and address quality concerns. Similarly, sales trends indicating customer churn risks helps leaders course correct retention activities before losing accounts. Across functions, centralized analytics sharply accelerate data-to-decisions velocity.

Bombarded with data, most companies starve for insights. The principles above trace an evolution whereby savvy analytics helps sales operations leaders progress from observing isolated facts to unlocking interconnected insights that fundamentally upgrade strategic thinking and outcomes. Converting raw data into actions – this shift holds the power to redefine what is possible.

Why Are Data Insights Important?

At its core, data insights are the gems waiting to be discovered within the vast realm of information. Imagine having a treasure map—your data—and finding the key spots that unlock hidden opportunities. When you make the right plans and choices guided by these insights, you set the stage for a business evolution.

Discovering insights is just the beginning; the real magic happens when you turn these revelations into actions. From understanding your audience's needs to optimizing processes, every insight is a stepping stone to tangible business improvements and growth.

Data Insights Allow More Informed Decisions

The rationale behind building analytics capabilities rests in the pursuit of superior insights to drive better choices. Whether navigating macro-level revenue, profitability and cash flow decisions or mi-

cro-level determinations around tactical areas like promotional campaigns, data-driven insights mitigate risks and reveal opportunities
otherwise invisible. Analytics shine a spotlight to guide resolution of
strategic issues and process problems.

Adopt Visual Analytics to Discover Patterns

Critical thinking with data involves uncovering influential patterns,
trends and relationships among numbers rather than simply reporting
figures. Visual analytics approaches transform datasets into intuitive
graphs, charts and dashboards designed to highlight key variability's.
For example, sales managers gain visibility into churn risks by interacting with customer loyalty metrics versus static retention rate tables.
Intuitive data exploration unlocks deeper insights.

Insights Should Align to Business Priorities

Relevance represents a pivotal litmus test when assessing the value
of unearthed insights. If uncovered patterns fail to provide direct,
actionable inputs into solving sales operations priorities around revenue growth, cost control or experience optimization, analytics efforts deliver minimal returns. For example, JPMorgan Chase measures analytics impact based on the ability for business leaders to implement improvements rooted in more informed perspectives of customer journeys. Analytics not activism acceleration through insights
grounded in strategic goals.

Present Insights as Compelling Visual Stories

Raw data frenzies often overwhelm rather than enlighten decisions.
Representing insights visually through graphs, charts and dashboards
conveys clarity and focus otherwise daunting lists of figures lack. Further, visual aesthetics lend increased stickiness for recalling crucial
intelligence learned earlier.

With the exponential growth in enterprise data, sales operations
is central to unlocking value by delivering relevant, activated insights

that focus strategic decisions and lead to better business outcomes. By honing your analytics acumen as an insight hunter, data detective and analytics activist, you empower impactful choices relying on intelligence - not intuition. Rather than passively gathering data, proactively develop key questions you want answered to guide your analytics strategy. Identify the specific insights that would be most valuable in informing executive strategies, regional targeting, resource allocation, and more. Utilize advanced analytics tools and statistical models to thoroughly investigate datasets, uncovering hidden patterns and relationships between factors influencing sales.

Uncover Patterns And Trends

Transforming raw data into strategic insights represents both a science and art form. While scrutinizing datasets, spotting variabilities and validating correlations seems straightforward, avoiding false or misleading interpretations requires equal parts analytics tradecraft, business acumen and leadership engagement. This discussion provides helpful principles to consider when working to extract and activate insights across sales operations.

Uncover Performance Changes and Root Causes

Foundational analytics involves meticulously scrutinizing data feeds to pinpoint changes over time, gaps across products or business units, and subgroup behaviors. For instance, customer churn metrics might reveal lower loyalty risks across certain geographies or customer cohorts. Spotting divergent outcomes compels inquiry into root causes driving the results. However, ambiguous statistical correlations or false assumptions often masquerade as factual insights. Rigorously validate suspected patterns and hypotheses through multi-dimensional analysis before drawing conclusions.

Incorporate Historical Data to Enrich Context

Reviewing longitudinal information, whether multi-year crime statistics or periodic sales records, greatly sharpens analytical context to enrich current insights. Analyzing historical performance, trends and seasonal impacts allows constructing trend-based projections to inform likely future outcomes. For example, factoring in prior holiday return rates by product line allows reasonably forecasting upcoming post-holiday effects. Anchoring analytics in empirical realities boosts contextual relevance.

Connect Insights Across Data Feeds to Expose Problems

Functional information siloes often constrain analysis, whereas connecting related metrics from across management systems and customer channels exposes fuller context. For instance, combining technician turnover analytics from HR platforms with historical recruiting data reveals how challenges sourcing talent manifest in higher vacancy rates and service delays. Cross-referencing data feeds interlinks issues to inform root cause priorities.

Insights Demand Activation Not Just Discovery

Collecting and reviewing data delivers negligible value absent integrating findings into decisions and initiatives that meaningfully advance revenue, efficiency and experience. For example, insights exposing alarming surges in inventory waste could compel executives to implement food rescue nonprofit partnerships to address needs sustainably. Construct narratives, share dashboards and publish visuals that spur leadership to action.

As more data becomes available, it can improve business strategy, but only if the data gives helpful insights. Good analysis means not mixing up things that aren't really related, looking at the full business situation, combining different data to see the whole picture, and making sure leaders use the insights to make decisions. Those principles are key to get value from the money spent on analytics. The analysis should uncover sales, marketing, and product trends and connections in the detailed data, showing where results fall short or could improve. Then, act on the insights by directly linking them to planning across departments. Always track outcomes from data-based choices to ensure accountability.

Key Takeaways

- Evolve from passive data reporting to uncovering influential patterns, connections and root causes behind the numbers.

- Leverage visual analytics approaches to transform datasets into intuitive graphs and dashboards that highlight variability.

- Activate insights by directly linking findings to strategies, decisions and execution across departments. Continually track outcomes.

- Centralize analytics platforms to break down information silos and power enterprise-wide data sharing that accelerates time-to-insight.

- Validate suspected patterns across multiple data dimensions to avoid false or misleading interpretations not grounded in empirical facts.

- Incorporate historical information to establish trend-lines and enrich analytical context to inform projections.

- Present insights through compelling visual narratives and

stories that focus leaders and compel actions, not just passive digestion.

Chapter 4
Foundations of Data Visualization

Turning complicated data into clear visual stories is an important strategic skill. Effective data visualization makes insights easier to understand and remember, which improves decision making. This article introduces core ideas to keep in mind when using charts, graphs and dashboards to share key findings from detailed data.

At its heart, data visualization is a communication tool to guide strategy and choices by having people grasp information faster. Well-designed visuals present sophisticated analysis in simple ways everyone can understand, with more impact and memory than wordy reports. For example, a color-coded map showing regional product sales differences gives more useful insights than giant data tables. Also, pictures reduce the thinking needed for complex issues.

However, basic charts fail to add value without the right context. Along with technical skills, statistical expertise and business know-how are vital to highlight important patterns in the details. Experienced analysts, for instance, put sales metrics in perspective by factoring in broader economic conditions when judging performance.

The accuracy, clarity and meaningful encoding concepts covered here build this critical perspective.

Data visualization helps sales operations drive faster, data-based decisions across the company, by translating raw data into accessible insights to improve outcomes. Dashboards revealing widening profit gaps among customer categories, for instance, allow leaders to fix loyalty programs based on facts before losses grow. The principles and best practices discussed teach sales managers to apply visualization tools in sharpening choices.

But producing purposeful graphs and charts takes work to avoid common pitfalls. Be selective in determining supporting metrics and key subgroup analyses, preventing overcomplicated outputs that overwhelm audiences with excessive or superficial information. Additionally, train end-users in properly deciphering encodings like color scales so findings get interpreted correctly.

Importantly, make analytics explorable through interactive displays. Empower colleagues to drill down into the underlying data, adjust parameters like time frames and extract customized cuts. Dynamic visibility across multiple lenses exposes deeper insights.

Still, flashy visuals with lots of filters can distract from main takeaways without clear structure and messaging. Leading dashboards feature thoughtful composition guiding viewers through information flow via thoughtful sequencing, logical layouts and signals highlighting noteworthy patterns. For example, opening with a one-page executive overview establishes focus before diving into operational details.

In sales operations, data visualization elevates communication while expediting fact-based decision making. Transforming complex datasets into intuitive graphics makes insights more accessible for driving strategy. Following core principles around accuracy, clarity and meaningful encodings allows building high-impact visuals that motivate positive changes.

The Expanding Role of Data Visualization

With exponential growth in data, sales operations leaders often need visual analytics to highlight important patterns and trends within complex information to guide strategy and decisions. Interactive data visualizations make insights easier to understand and remember based on thorough analysis. Here are key principles on using data visualization to accelerate and upgrade decision-making:

Visualizations Spot Key Factors Among Complexity

Fundamentally, data visualization streamlines convoluted datasets down to the most influential relationships and variabilities. For instance, regional sales heatmaps instantly spotlight high and low performing products lines. With interactive charts, you can drill down by added factors like customer segments, seasons or economic conditions to see what drives results. Pictures improve understanding of complicated business issues over text-heavy reporting.

Patterns Expose Risks and Opportunities

Spotting abnormalities and outliers is a vital analytical skill that visualization assists. Unusual data points often show underlying weaknesses or gaps impeding performance. For example, spikes in customer turnover may signal product flaws or service bottlenecks needing quick action. Visual analysis shines a light on divergence and improves catching anomalies across massive datasets too enormous to assess manually.

Visuals Boost Recall and Persuasion

Additionally, aesthetically striking and intuitive visuals lift comprehension, learning and memory of insights from analysis rather than dry statistics. Retention skyrockets when key takeaways get etched into recollection through compelling data stories. Moreover, evidence-based visualization sways decision makers to address pressing issues or prospects.

Interactivity Allows Exploration from New Angles

Static reporting only lets you assess business matters from pre-set viewpoints, while interactive dashboards empower end users to reshape perspectives on the fly. Changing filters, variables and visualizations drives an exploration cycle where discoveries happen progressively. Altering data representation highlights insights. For instance, toggling sales metrics from geographic maps to customer concentration heat grids may uncover profitable niches.

Benchmarking Puts Performance in Context

Vital context gets lost when judging performance in a vacuum without historical comparisons. Contrast sales results, pipeline velocity or forecast accuracy against prior periods using benchmark indicators. For example, unusually high customer loss may seem concerning but pale versus recession-related challenges last year. Benchmarking grounds reactive instincts in factual realities.

Acting on Insights Counts More Than Visuals

Importantly, visualization aims to accelerate translating insights into actions through faster data processing, not just basic presentation. If product return analysis uncovers quality issues from particular manufacturers, for instance, visual alerts could prompt supply chain leaders to switch vendors. Similarly, eroding loyalty risks revealed by analytics should trigger proactive retention initiatives. For sales operations, value requires acting on intelligence.

Intuitive visualizations dispel confusion, speed pattern finding, boost recollection and accelerate data-driven decisions. As data and analytics complexity increases across sales operations, applying visualization, benchmarking and storytelling tools separates leaders who can influence strategically from those chasing statistics.

Effective and Intuitive Visualization of Data

For sales operations, fast-growing data makes visualizing insights more vital for easy understanding and recall. Graph mastery quickens grasping key information to persuade and spark decisions. This covers core design ideas and best practices to optimize clarity when presenting complex data. The goal is intuitive pictures that improve comprehension to drive outcomes from intelligence, not just statistics. Focus visuals on revealing key trends, gaps and opportunities then push activation through aligned decisions across departments.

Champion User-Centered Design

User-centricity seems obvious yet often gets overlooked when data teams prioritize showcasing technical prowess over resolving viewer needs. Incorporating human-centered design (HCD) principles counteracts these pitfalls through continual user feedback incorporation across visualization efforts.

- Conduct empathy mapping to understand audience priorities, challenges and preferences.

- Iterate interactive prototype visuals based on usage testing observations.

- Validate final designs against cognitive comprehension and aesthetic appeal criteria.

For example, customer service teams may require intuitive dashboards monitoring sentiment changes and complaint trends. Tailor solutions resonating with their roles, analytical maturity and visual consumption patterns. HCD-rooted designs feel familiar, inviting engagement over intimidation.

Reduce Complexity While Balancing Depth

The most common pitfall involves overloading screens with intricate graphics or dense metric details that inhibit comprehension. Lead with simplicity - spotlight only the most influential insights using easy-to-decode visuals and eliminate embellishments that distract from core narratives. Convey overview awareness prominently before navigating into granular specifics.

- Prominently display surface level insights for initial consumption.

- Use slide partitioning and progressive disclosure techniques to manage complexity.

- Incorporate interactive filters and drill downs enabling user-driven deep dives.

Well-designed analysis both informs and empowers without overwhelming. Annotations, whitespace and visual hierarchy draw attention across prioritized elements to reinforce data stories. Savvy complexity balancing upgrades clarity.

Boost Memorability Through Strategic Emphasis

Leverage visual contrast techniques to spotlight crucial insights for recall while reducing contextual noise. For example:

- Saturate colors on underperforming KPI bars across muted charts.

- Embrace generous whitespace to focus processing on key variabilities.

Such emphasis guides visual journeys, directing observations across targeted messaging. Additionally, consistency in chart types, icons and palettes improves information retention as audiences become fluent with recurring encodings.

Establish Narrative Flow Through Intentional Sequencing

Arrange visuals to logically guide viewers across core narratives rather than disjointed facts. Sequence images to first establish background awareness and then spotlight important variability's that shape emerging insights. For example:

- Introduce category-level sales results visually before diving into regional views.

- Structure visuals to align with narrative arcs building towards conclusions.

Combined with consistent theming, purposeful sequencing weaves fragmented graphics into intuitive stories flowing naturally towards key discoveries. Guide journeys, don't distract.

Cultivate Trust with Credibility Cues

Even perfectly designed visuals fail their purpose if audiences doubt data legitimacy or objectivity. Fortunately, several subtle design moves help boost credibility:

- Attribute data sources and update timestamps directly within frames.

- Maintain consistent currency symbols, percentages and formats across views.

- Eliminate elements susceptible to misinterpretation or manipulation allegations.

Transparent lineage and measurement integrity cues foster viewer confidence in underlying analytics. Trusted insights more effectively influence strategies backed by evidence instead of assumptions.

Uphold Accuracy and Representation Ethics

Beyond aesthetics, Sales Operations leaders carry immense responsibility ensuring analytical integrity and representation ethics central to data-driven cultures:

- Clearly label visual axes and data points for accurate interpretation.

- Eliminate misleading visual elements distorting reality.

- Maintain appropriate scales, baselines and benchmarking context.

While data manipulation often intends turbocharging performance rather than malicious deception, the outcomes ravage trust and leadership credibility once exposed. Symbols and figures must uphold factual accuracy.

Prioritize Responsiveness Across Presentation Mediums

With remote and mobile fluency now mission-critical, visualizations must transcend static slides. Responsive capabilities allow adaptable rendering optimized across varied screens and devices:

- Web-based dashboards resize gracefully on laptops, tablets and smartphones.

- Export presentations using tablet-friendly dimensions if distributing offline.

Responsiveness empowers both dynamically customized views for different leaders and contexts as well as universal access unchained from infrastructure constraints.

The principles and practices above demonstrate how foundational fluency in clarity, alignment, credibility and responsibility begets advanced data visualization prowess even amidst exponentially proliferating data complexity. Savvy sales operations leaders will realize success in driving organization change and sales success relies on creatively converting raw metrics into intuitive visual guidance. This in turn propels better decisions through actionable insights.

Choosing Visuals for Your Data

The key to building data fluency involves strategically translating metrics into graphical shapes, colors, sizes and positions that spotlight meaningful patterns across datasets. Mastering visualization encoding entails matching robust encodings to data types and analytical objectives to accentuate key insights, persuade audiences and compose multidimensional narratives all while upholding integrity principles.

Understand Visualization Options Through Data Types

Getting started rests on cataloging visualization options available based on categorical, temporal, hierarchical, relational, distributional and geospatial data types frequently analyzed in sales operations contexts.

Categorical Data Visualizations

- Bar charts spotlight comparisons across qualitative groupings like product lines, market segments or brands using rectangular bars of varying lengths aligned to values.

- Pie charts highlight proportional contributions in circular format divided into categorized "slices".

- Dot plots position circles in series to illustrate concentrations and distributions across groups. Sizing by value adds additional insight.

Time Series Data Visualizations

- Line charts connect periodic measurements over time to showcase trends, trajectory changes and forecasting.

- Area charts build on line charts using shading between axis and line integrals to represent cumulative values over time.

- Gantt charts use horizontal bar segments placed along a calendar to illustrate project timelines and scheduling interdependencies through positioning and alignments.

Hierarchical Data Visualizations

- Tree maps nest rectangular segmentation recursively to depict relative proportional contributions hierarchically.

- Dependency wheels show nested values through concentric rings ordered inside-out by level showing both individual and roll-up contributions.

- Sunburst charts layer inner-to-outer hierarchical rings as arcs scaled proportionally to totals.

Distribution Data Visualizations

- Histograms group continuous data values into bins and draw bars representing frequencies of observations falling within bin ranges to spotlight shape and positioning of variability concentrations.

- Density plots use continuous, smooth lines to illustrate value distribution patterns, concentrating attention on curve peaks, symmetry, skewing and other insights impossible to spot in histograms.

- Box-and-whisker plots summarize distribution by displaying median, upper/lower quartiles and outlier cutoff lines concisely within a visually compact yet information-rich format.

Relational Data Visualizations

- Scatter plots position circles mapping measurements on X-Y axes to showcase correlations, clusters, exceptions and outliers through location, grouping and directional patterns.

- Heatmaps overlay color gradation onto two-dimensional data grids allowing spotting densities, intensities and magnitudes within specific regions of data ranges.

- Network diagrams link related nodes visually to highlight interconnectivity, flow and groupings. Directionality, color and styling encode additional meaning.

Geospatial Data Visualizations

- Choropleth maps divide geographical regions into shaded areas encoding values through color saturations such that higher intensities reflect larger measurement levels and vice versa.

- Dot density maps scatter bubbles across regions with concentrations representing proportions, averages and totals associated with positioning. Colors can encode additional variables.

- Flow maps overlay arrow lines onto regions with widths proportional to movement from origin to destination locations. Directionality and color heighten insights.

Combine Visualizations to Layer Insights

Data narratives often weave together multiple visual metaphors across layouts using technique. Ideally this should pair aligned objectives to analytical objectives. For example:

- Blend choropleth and dot density maps to tie regional insights to distribution awareness.

- Connect seasonal trendlines with correlation scatter plots to add statistical validity.

- Superimpose target benchmarks onto performance charts to contextualize status.

Strategic encoding orchestration makes the whole insight greater than the sum of the parts by chaining complementary representations into an aligned story.

Innovate Through Advanced and Interactive Techniques

While foundational encodings are sufficient for many recurring reports and dashboards, scenarios involving multilayered complexity, predictive modeling and real-time monitoring often necessitate innovative ways of presenting data.

Interactive Drill-Downs

- Enable viewer-driven filtering and investigation by building hierarchy-aware visualizations supporting on-demand drilldowns to underlying details.

- Empower self-service visual query capabilities through faceted search options and adaptable business logic.

Predictive Forecasting Plots

- Extend time-series visualizations into future periods using forecasting models to provide predictive trajectory views based on trend algorithm outputs.

- Shade prediction range bands around baseline estimates to communicate certainty qualifications.

Sparkline Element Integration

- Sparklines miniaturize charts to occupy small spaces while retaining trend shapes and thus work elegantly blended into reporting tables, dashboards and applications to encode additional context.

- For example, transaction tables listing customer purchases by date could append miniature line charts visualizing seasonal sales patterns or projecting returns.

Interactive Benchmarks

- Make benchmark lines or bands manipulatable to test performance at various goal thresholds.

- For instance, sales managers might slide targets to more ambitious levels while revenue charts instantly reconfigure gap calculations.

Animation and Motion

- Animate visual analytics by programmatically transitioning states over time rather than via discrete static slides to demonstrate process flows.

- For example, show geospatial data evolutions across historical periods using time-lapse mappings to represent trends and trajectory changes impacting current states.

Responsiveness and Portability
- Mobile readiness through auto-resizing and restructuring visualizations for ideal visibility across varied devices counters access barriers.

- Cloud hosting also enables audience-tailored distribution via web links, embedded integration or exportable downloads compatible with business intelligence tools leveraged across stakeholders.

The combinations of encodings possible through thoughtful selection, arrangement, innovation and responsiveness are endless. Mastery Across these knowledge areas separates technically proficient analysts from transformational data storytellers who make the complex feel simple and inform strategies through clarity.

Uphold Accessibility, Accuracy and Integrity

However, with the boundless possibility unlocked by visuals lies additional accountability, especially around ethical obligations. Sales operations managers carry the responsibility of ensuring analytical integrity and representation of principles. Here are some best practice guidelines:

Design For Universal Accessibility

- Employ color palettes compatible with color blindness or low vision conditions.

- Provide Options for screen reader integration and keyboard navigation access to prevent exclusion.

Label Judiciously to Prevent Misinterpretation
- Clearly label visual axes, baselines, benchmarks and data points for accurate decoding.

- Call attention to context like seasonality effects that explain perceived variability.

Scrutinize for Distortion Risks
- Eliminate embellishments introducing ambiguity or proportions misalignment.

- Ask critical questions to confirm conclusions align to true representations before finalizing.

What matters most, even more than eye-catching data pictures, is representing information fairly, so everyone can understand it and trust that it's valid. Without first establishing viewer confidence through transparency and integrity, the fanciest graphs fail their purpose.

As data complexity grows across sales systems, knowing how to translate numbers into easy-to-grasp visuals, using good design rules and analytical care, separates advanced analytics teams. Real wisdom is converting fragmented metrics into visual guidance enabling all leaders to make wiser, ethical, evidence-based calls through human-focused data stories.

The goal is to turn detailed information into strategic insights that make sense through clear visuals for different audiences. Keep things straightforward rather than chasing statistics that don't resonate. Focus visualization on revealing key trends, gaps and opportunities to drive better decisions across the company.

Key Takeaways

- Visualizations streamline complex data into intuitive graphs and charts that spotlight key patterns, risks, gaps and opportunities.

- Interactive dashboards empower end users to reshape visual perspectives and drill into details to expose insights.

- Use aesthetics, contrast and annotations that draw attention to guide narrative flow across core insights for better recall.

- Uphold representation ethics and analytical integrity through accurate labels, baselines and scales to build viewer trust.

- Combine complementary chart types to layer multivariate insights more impactfully than isolated statistics.

- Innovate using drilldowns, predictive plots, sparklines and motion to engage audiences with multifaceted data stories.

- Above all, focus visuals on revealing trends and variability's that drive aligned planning and decisions, leading to business improvements.

Chapter 5

The Impact of Data-Driven Stories

D ata visuals inform, but stories inspire action. Sales operations can use narratives to make an emotional connection, sparking productive talks and better decisions. Good storytelling understands the data but focuses on people. It translates dry insights into real meaning that drives change. The goal is continuing a cycle – turn data into insights, insights into actions through stories, actions into outcomes, outcomes into new data. Rinse and repeat. When analysis tells a compelling tale, leaders don't just listen. They act.

What are Data Stories?

Data storytelling means framing insights inside compelling narratives that simplify complexity and drive change. For sales operations dealing with exploding data, intuitive stories make statistics stick, convince and prompt action. Crafting useful tales encompasses both science and artistry. This covers why data narratives provide vital context, how to boost engagement, and tips to start adding stories across reporting.

The goal is continuing the cycle – turn data into insights, insights into actions through stories, actions into outcomes, outcomes into new data. Rinse and repeat.

Stories Add Crucial Context to Raw Data

At its core, data storytelling contextualizes data, statistics, and figures into insightful narratives explaining why numbers change over time and why those variabilities matter. For example, while showcasing rising product returns quarter-over-quarter using charts proves straightforward, spotlighting the underlying quality deficiencies requires comprehensive narratives tracing nuances from customer complaints to production line failures. Stories weave isolated signals into cohesive tapes together to upgrade understanding.

Further, academic research affirms narratives boost comprehension and recall radically better than statistics alone as the structural elements characteristic of stories—plot progression, contextual framing and informational flow—resonate innately with human cognition. In chaotic informational landscapes, stories act as indispensable filters separating signals from noise.

Core Elements: Data, Visuals and Narrative Flow

Effective data stories comprise three central elements working in harmony:

- Raw data elements reveal the tangible "what" is happening.

- Visual representations demonstrate the most crucial changes.

- Narratives contextualize observations into insights explaining why variabilities matter and what should happen next.

For example, regional executive dashboards may showcase sales fig-ures, include maps highlighting overperforming areas and craft ac-companying captions tracing macroeconomic tailwinds influencing the results. Stories build bridges between discovery and action.

Inspire Change Through Context and Simplicity

Data storytelling aims beyond simply documenting trends through better visuals. The purpose involves contextualizing complex ideas into simplified narratives that inspire change and upgrade decision making. For example, while showcasing customer loyalty metrics eroding quarterly makes issues tangible, crafting a narrative about the underlying experiences causing disaffection compels leaders to ur-gently rethink retention efforts. Facts evidence. Stories persuade.

Begin Building Data Narrative Skills

For analytic professionals seeking to elevate reporting influence, basic tips like learning story mapping frameworks, watching exem-plars from leaders like Accenture and Alberto Cairo, and practicing through informal blog or newsletter opportunities represent great starting points to hone nascent skills. Quick wins establish founda-tions to embed storytelling broadly across data-driven cultures and high-impact deliverables where decision outcomes rest in the balance.

Start Small by Contextualizing Known Insights

When getting started, begin practicing contextualizing known trends through hypothetical framed narratives for low-risk refine-ments rather than tackling highly visible presentations lacking experi-ence. For example, augment basic sales reports with market condition factors that could explain performance challenges. These small addi-tions accrue foundational skills quicker through repetition.

Incorporate More Visualizations to Demonstrate Changes

As confidence builds, interweave visual storyline elements like charts spotlighting sales variability across regions or products last quarter. As larger time-series accrue, trace performance historically to establish plausibility of current changes as part of more elaborate narration. Basic visualization integration dramatically upgrades narrative impact.

Graduate to Interactive Dashboards Enabling Storytelling

Mature data storytelling methods eventually leverage interactive dashboards that empower customized exploration by decision-makers to delve across various insights aspects through immersive visibility. For instance, dynamic interfaces could trace customer churn risk factors across multiple levels from individual dissatisfaction drivers to segment-wide trends. Interactivity promotes engagement and lasts beyond presentations.

Data storytelling weaves credible visual evidence into simplified narratives upgrading comprehension, memorability and actionability of complex analytics. For sales operations leaders navigating accelerating information complexity across customers, performance indicators and macro-conditions, eloquent data narrative capabilities increasingly dictate influence. Facts enlighten, but stories compel.

Appealing to Emotions and Building Connections

Trustworthy data visuals and easy-to-grasp statistics are key parts of intuitive narratives, but lasting stories also connect emotionally to convince minds and hearts. Strategically adding empathy, relatability and links to values transforms dry data into inspiring calls for change. Stories that resonate emotionally as well as logically stick with audiences longer while bringing more people onboard. The goal is continuing the cycle – turn data into insights, insights into actions through stories, actions into outcomes, outcomes into new data.

Emphasize Emotional Resonance in Stories

Academic studies reveal emotionally resonant narratives drastically amplify the influence from messaging through enhanced memorability and motivation. For example, fundraising campaigns highlighting statistical realities of poverty often fade quickly from memory. Meanwhile, stories spotlighting individual beneficiaries more than double contributions as personal connectivity elicits empathy that transcends numbness from overwhelming numbers and statistics.

This relatability fuels caring that ultimately spurs the desired action, whether alleviating suffering or pursuing growth opportunities. The key is crafting narratives that create experiential understanding through character-driven plotlines instead of distant factual awareness alone. Help audiences feel the frustrations from dropping loyalty or the hopes surrounding an emerging customer segment through strategic empathy.

Humanize Data Through Examples That Relate

Transitioning analytics from vague aggregation reporting into clarity involves humanizing datasets to unlock relatability.

Traditional analytics reporting often focuses heavily on numbers in aggregate - totals, percentages, averages and other statistical summaries across large groups like customers, sales territories, products lines, etc. While mathematically accurate, looking at groups rather than individuals can dehumanize data and make it feel abstract, overwhelming or disconnected from real life.

Humanizing data means transitioning from broad statistical reporting to perspectives that promote relatability and meaning by putting a "human face" on figures whenever appropriate. For example, highlighting personalized customer insights through persona profiles or selective case study examples makes engagement data feel more intimate. Explaining regional sales variances through on-the-ground vignettes makes performance metrics resonate at a visceral level. Even naming advanced algorithmic models after key intentions makes automated intelligence seem friendlier.

The key is not ignoring rigorous analytics principles - accuracy always remains paramount - but rather judiciously focusing data presentations, visuals and narratives toward driving clarity for audiences by promoting understanding and emotional connections with key insights derived from complex datasets. The payoff comes through relatability translating to engagement, recall and actionability based on tying data and decisions to human experiences.

For instance, present customer churn rates alongside quoted anecdotes from exit interviews bringing visibility into the precise pain points propelling abandonment mentioned recurrently. This granularity sticks in memories far longer as personalities emerge from figures through stories.

Further, incorporate photographic element whenever possible showing real employees or customers representative of target groups discussed across data narratives. Putting faces alongside facts fuses logical and emotional intrigue that compels engagement across both dimensions.

Connect Observations to Values and Priorities

Data stories have the most impact when the insights connect to the values, priorities and goals that audiences already believe are important. Strategic framing shows how data outputs support achieving the results people really care about, like increasing revenue, improving customer retention, or boosting service. This builds common ground and trust faster than asking people to take on new perspectives.

For example, an analysis about changes in customer loyalty levels over the past year will seem abstract to many leaders focused on hitting revenue growth targets. However, framing the same insights around projecting how declining loyalty threatens revenue goals makes the intelligence feel indispensable. The data itself doesn't change, but linking revelations directly to executives' existing key objectives encourages adoption and action based on aligning with pre-existing motivations.

Similarly, surface level reporting on page views, time spent, and clicks provide limited value. But analytics leveraging the same datasets to showcase how proposed improvements to the self-service portal can accelerate problem resolution and lift customer satisfaction scores will capture attention. The data supports executives already concentrating on customer retention over those focused purely on operational metrics.

Updating statistics with data stories replaces information overload with simplified visuals. This marks only the starting point for intuitive data stories that persuade decisions through lasting emotional connections. Strategically incorporating relatable examples and empathy help important priorities come alive for audiences, while catalyzing emotional investment that ignites action.

Using Data Storytelling to Direct Focus and Drive Understanding

Well-crafted data-driven stories ground abstract numbers in real-world meaning, highlight key events for action, and counter resistance to new insights. Here are practical tips for using compelling narratives to guide attention and alignment around analytics.

An impactful data story provides more than just statistics. By emphasizing critical moments and explaining their significance, you direct audience focus towards key events and insights needing action. For example, highlighting an unusual dip in website conversion rates, describing the revenue implications, and noting a recent site redesign as a likely cause focuses attention on an issue to address. Logically building one data revelation upon another also sustains engagement while moving readers towards key takeaways. Consider how to frame data as an intriguing story leading audiences to intended conclusions.

A key data storytelling benefit is reshaping prevailing internal narratives that breed denial, doubt or dismissal of analytics revelations. We all interpret information through ingrained stories and assumptions. When data challenges existing narratives, rejection often results. Facts alone rarely break this resistance. However, stories aligning with audience beliefs while opening minds to new possibilities can enable adopting insights from the data. First seek to understand internal narratives, then build a sympathetic story finding common ground between different viewpoints. With care for others' perspectives, data can compel change even in rigid mindsets.

These are some best practices for directing focus and driving understanding:

Identify Key Events and Context

- Spot unusual swings in metrics and describe their tangible impact

- Explain potential causes to focus attention and direct next steps

- Ensure context links data to real-world meaning and significance

Craft Logical, Escalating Narratives

- Sequence data revelations to build towards key takeaways

- Use storytelling techniques like plot trajectories to sustain engagement

- Structure flows to guide audiences to intended conclusions

Align with Internal Perspectives

- Recognize preexisting narratives that may breed resistance

- Find common ground between different vantage points

- Leverage areas of agreement to open minds to fresh insights

In summary, excellent data storytelling requires more than basic metrics. Guide understanding by spotlighting pivotal events, providing real-world context, and structuring logically flowing narratives. Additionally, leverage thoughtful stories to reshape stubborn perspectives impeding necessary decisions. With care to connect insights to audience beliefs, analytics can prompt change through credible, contextualized tales. Pay attention to both data patterns and accompanying stories to enable high-impact communication that directs focus and drives informed, aligned action.

Prompting Discussions and Stimulation of Ideas

With thoughtful framing, analytics can prompt conversations, participation, and scenario planning rather than just providing static conclusions. As a sales operations leader, you can leverage narrative elements such as open-ended framing, interactive visuals, and hypothetical situations to spark new insights from your teams. These are some approaches to data narratives that engage audiences and stimulate the exchange of ideas and strategy.

Framing Narratives to Invite Discussion

Clever analysts can always find meaningful facts and figures to share. However, compelling analytics leaders also understand that the most significant revelations result from active discourse prompted by thoughtful reporting. Avoid the temptation to view data stories as opportunities to broadcast rigid statistical conclusions. Instead, intentionally craft narratives with room for audiences to interpret implications, debate alternatives, and build upon presented information. For example, framing conversion rate declines as a potential "signal of changing market expectations" invites consideration of underlying causes driving observed data trends. Interactive discussions naturally emerge from open-ended narratives that reject definitive statements in favor of collective sensemaking.

Driving Participation through Interactive Storytelling

The most engaging data stories feel like a conversation rather than a lecture. Interactive elements provide openings for audiences to directly participate in narrative development. Use visual components like charts, graphs, and info graphics linked to underlying analytics to let stakeholders explore implications at their own pace. Ask strategic questions at key moments rather than just stating conclusions to encourage responsive dialogue. Employ polls, whiteboard collaboration, and on-screen annotations so teams can immerse themselves in data interpretation. Enable hands-on participation to turn static reporting into an activity that drives critical thinking and creativity from your audience.

Incorporating Scenarios for Innovation

Data narratives can spur new ideas and strategy by incorporating hypothetical scenarios to prompt reflective discussions. After establishing essential data trends, pose "what if" situations related to product launches, economic events, emerging competitors or other potential market disruptions. For example, analytics around conversion rates by product line may inform scenarios around discontinuing underperforming segments or targeting COPY higher-margin offerings. Avoid scenarios feeling like far-fetched speculation by grounding them in logical extensions of observed data. Ultimately, thoughtful conjecture spurs exchanges that uncover innovative opportunities and strategies grounded in analytics rather than abstract guesswork.

Crafting Visuals for Storytelling Impact

Annotative layers, logical sequence and thematic alignment of data visuals with key messaging all contribute to heightened engagement, understanding and actionability for intended audiences. As a sales operations leader responsible for communicating insights from analytics, you have a prime opportunity to evolve reporting beyond standalone charts, graphs and tables. By deliberately incorporating explanatory context, logical flow and consistent themes into data representations, you enable intuitive comprehension that drives strategic outcomes.

Enhancing Data Visuals through Contextual Annotations

Even insightful data visualizations benefit immensely from embedded story elements that annotate graphics to highlight contextual significance, pivot points and implications warranting action. Call out relevant events such as short-term sales surges and specify associated marketing initiatives or product releases as likely drivers. Identify periods of declining performance and annotate external factors like economic downturns that may have influenced observed trends. Provide explanatory detail directly within data representations to intuitively guide viewer focus while adding clarity regarding causes, effects and appropriate responses based on depicted analytics.

Structuring Cohesive Data Narratives

The sequence and progression of data visuals can either logically build a cohesive narrative or present disjointed graphics with no interconnected meaning. Purposefully arrange visualizations to first establish foundational data then advance step-by-step through insightful trends and accompanying events towards key takeaways. Align explanatory annotations within each graphic to reinforce the overarching narrative as audiences progress through the data story. Maintain consistent cause-and-effect messaging across visuals tied to business goals so that data representations work in concert rather than isolation to convey actionable final conclusions.

Incorporating Diverse Perspectives

While a logically structured narrative prevents visuals from seeming disconnected, excessive top-down storytelling can also limit interpretations to a single narrow perspective. Seek direct input from other data stakeholders when annotating graphics or developing explanatory data flows. Fresh sets of eyes typically notice different trends, contextual factors or conclusions that data may suggest. Embrace collaborative storytelling to intentional incorporate diverse viewpoints into annotated visuals and interwoven narrative elements. Inputs from analysts, operations and even frontline roles create data stories that speak to broader audiences while still maintaining cohesive explanatory progressions.

Measuring the Effectiveness of Data-Driven Stories

The true power of data-driven storytelling depends on a commitment to continual optimization rather than isolated reporting. Gathering stakeholder feedback, tracking quantitative metrics, iterating narrative techniques, and aligning analytics narratives with core business objectives fuels ongoing improvements and maximized decision-making impact. As a sales operations leader accountable for communicating insights, prioritize credible processes for regularly assessing and refining your data storytelling strategy.

Soliciting Responsive Feedback

The best data stories resonate with target audiences, prompting cognitive shifts and changes in strategic direction. But without constructive feedback channels, the isolated reporting role lacks visibility into how narratives actually land with recipients. Establish open comment forms, facilitated discussions, and user interviews to collect experiential insights around engagement, relevance and impact of analytics narratives. Gather data on stand out elements as well as confusing aspects requiring clarification so future iterations better speak to listener priorities. Regular feedback processes, even simple post-report surveys, provide the user perspectives essential for heightening communicative influence through intentional story tuning.

Tracking Quantitative Measures

While subjective inputs highlight areas of refinement, quantitative metrics lend hard evidence on current data story effectiveness and opportunities for optimization. Strong starting metrics include narrative engagement (email open/click rates), content comprehension (quiz scores) and reporting mindshare (views, downloads and tool usage rates). Capture decision-maker sentiment through quick pre- and post-reporting polls. Over longer periods, factor strategy changes, process improvements and revenue growth attributable to data story insights. Quantifiable measures, filtered by reporting channel, audience segment and use case, guide A/B testing of explanatory annotations, narrative structures, delivery formats and other storytelling variables for continuous evidentiary improvement.

Iterating Based on Collective Insights

One-off data stories fail to fulfill their true potential without iteration leveraging feedback and metrics to heighten respondent resonance over time. No first draft narrative lands perfectly. But with reader/listener comments and quantified engagement data fueling incremental revisions across reporting touchpoints, future data stories more intuitively speak to audience priorities. The progression of narrative refinements – a sharpened analysis here, an explanatory annotation there – combines external perspectives with internal analytics into ever more polished data communication capable of capturing minds and redirecting strategy. Sustained iterations propel data storytelling maturity.

To keep improving data's ability to guide choices through stories, focus first on trustworthy processes ensuring analytics narratives match audience requirements and business needs. Establish regular feedback channels, track quantitative effectiveness measures, and make ongoing reporting upgrades based on insights gathered. This transforms stationary reporting into a dynamic engine to excel at data communication.

The key is continually gauging and evolving data storytelling based on evidence of what makes statistics meaningful for decision makers. For example, survey executives monthly on their top data concerns and perceived gaps that shape decisions. Plot effectiveness rates over time for different analytical frameworks at enabling data-driven choices. Look at narrative resonance across functions by tracking data visualization recall rates or monitoring verbal mentions in meetings.

Feed insights back into a systematic methodology for developing relatable data stories that stick. Enlist customer advisory panels to stress test explanations and eliminate confusion. Work cross-func-

tionally to address disconnected insights that inhibit organiza-
tion-wide strategy alignment. With iterations informed by collecting
mixed methods inputs around resonance and recall, reporting evolves
interactively towards communications excellence.

Overall, creating credible storytelling processes is crucial for lifting data's leadership influence through purposeful enhancements
grounded in audience feedback. Measure what makes statistics stick
then evolve narratives accordingly. Reliable improvements for translating numbers into meaningful stories that motivate change come
from evidence-based listening.

Key Takeaways

- Data stories add crucial context to raw statistics, making
  insights stickier, more convincing and actionable through
  narrative techniques.

- Build narratives using data, visuals and explanatory flow to
  spotlight key events and guide audiences to conclusions.

- Craft relatable stories with emotional resonance by humanizing data and connecting insights to audience values.

- Guide focus to key events by providing real-world significance and structuring logical plot progression that leads to
  takeaways.

- Use open-ended framing, interactivity and hypothetical scenarios to spark rich discussions and innovation from teams.

- Annotate visuals, sequence purposefully, gather diverse inputs and align to business goals to build intuitive data stories.

- Continually optimize storytelling by soliciting feedback, tracking engagement metrics and iterating based on evidence of narrative impact.

Chapter 6
How to Build a Data-Driven Story

It's tempting to think any data visualization naturally conveys an intriguing story or that overloading charts tells narratives well. However, compelling data-driven accounts demand more intentionality than these myths suggest. Let's debunk assumptions for clarity.

Myth 1: Data Visualizations Are Inherently Stories

A common pitfall equates charts and graphs with narrative accounts since both display figures aesthetically. However, isolated visuals lack a fundamental storytelling element – the contextual through-line tying details together to spotlight insights.

While quality data visualizations bring metrics to life, the surrounding narrative arc amplifies discoveries by integrating details into a focused spotlight. Powerful sequencing, explanatory frames and structured flow distinguish compelling data stories from fragmented visual depictions.

Myth 2: More Data and Visuals Captivate

Another misstep assumes overloading narratives with endless metrics and visuals strengthens resonance given the increased volume. Yet restraint and curation typically sharpen audience focus instead.

Excessive visuals and figures compete for limited attention, obscuring poignant insights worthy of spotlight amidst the commotion. Slicing clutter to showcase only supportive, contextualized data points clarifies relationships and highlights intended discoveries for comprehension and recall.

Debunking assumptions that all visuals tell stories or that more metrics mesmerize allows recalibrating expectations. While data visualizations serve as an indispensable medium for spotlighting key facts, the surrounding crafted narrative makes accounts truly shine by accentuating insights in ways fragmented visuals alone cannot.

Dispelling these myths makes space for data storytelling techniques that selectively amplify data's meaning beyond isolated imagery into resonant accounts purposefully woven with target insights.

Elements of a Data Story

Turning a bunch of scattered data points into a captivating story that drives good decisions requires tying the worlds of analytical facts and creative storytelling together. Strong data stories apply key tactics from both areas – they ground the explaining in quality data takeaways and blend engaging elements tailored for influencing sales leaders' choices.

Specifically, build logical, step-by-step flows focused on clarifying why trends and patterns in the data happened. Also blend in relatable settings, characters and plots that connect emotionally with your key audiences. Impactful data charts that direct attention to the most crucial metrics also simplify complicated quantitative relationships into intuitive light bulb moments.

Following storyline arcs allows each nugget to build anticipation toward the featured discoveries and calls-to-action to make changes. Artfully balance data-focused facts with dramatic flair. Making it relatable turns dry stats into stories that resonate.

By getting out in front of knowledge gaps and weaving analytical aha's together with narrative engagement, sales honchos can craft compelling data accounts. These convey intended points, spur better choices and unite outlooks across an organization. Harness the power of metrics wrapped in storytelling to produce stories that inform minds, inspire fresh thinking and kickstart positive change. Let artful data tales lead stakeholders toward more in-tune data-in-action decisions.

Data Foundation

A story's credibility stems from its underlying data quality. This is why it is important toeEnsure quantitative and qualitative information adheres to reliability, accuracy and transparency standards before determining suitability for spotlighting those facts as data stories.

Central Main Point: Every strong narrative aligns around a unifying main point or key insight. This core revelation provides purpose and prevents meandering accounts. Determine this destination before storyboarding begins.

Explanatory Focus: Go beyond dry data descriptions to clarify reasons behind trends and patterns discovered. Context illuminates meanings for analytical grasp to inform decisions.

Deliberate Sequencing: Structure supporting metrics to unveil in progressive, chronological order allowing gradual insight assimilation. Thoughtful flow facilitates comprehension and conclusion adoption.

Relatable Connections: Skillfully incorporate relevant cultural elements that resonate emotionally with target audiences to aid accessibility. People connect insights to human impacts.

These fundamental elements synergize quantitative and qualitative facets to produce compelling data accounts that deliver intended meanings and messages for adoption by sales operations decision-makers.

Data Storytelling Framework

Several integrated frameworks provide helpful narrative models for bringing data stories to life:

- **Introduction, Conflict, Resolution** – Structured account arcs including exposition, rising action and resolution maintain engagement while clearly conveying key messages.

- **Spotlight Impactful Metrics** - Curate measurements holding special meaning given goals and audience interests for prominence within sequence and visualization anchoring.

- **Surface Significant Deviations** – Illuminate data abnormalities and outliers to focus attention on gaps requiring realignment interventions.

- **Incorporate Cultural Touchstone** – Integrate organizational symbols, shared language and archetypes to increase resonance and reflections.

- **Address Knowledge Shortcomings** – Preemptively tackle potential areas of uncertainty or skepticism through explanatory and visual transparency.

Adapt these models to reinforce intentions as you customize data stories for sales operations influence across a spectrum of stakeholders and scenarios.

Building your Data Story

Building an impactful data story involves navigating two key phases: exploring data to unearth insights and explaining findings to motivate decisions. Effectively transitioning between these stages helps transform scattered data points into captivating narratives that drive change.

The exploration phase resembles an archaeological dig - combing through data seeking hidden gems. Create basic charts focused purely on spotting trends and anomalies rather than polished graphics. Dash through datasets iteratively, letting visuals speak patterns and deviations to guide your analysis.

These early visuals needn't impress external audiences - their role is illuminating insights for you as lead excavator. Expect twists as you challenge assumptions until a compelling gem emerges worth spotlighting.

The explanation phase shifts focus toward sharing featured discoveries through purposeful storytelling. Now adopt a teacher mindset - simplifying findings for those lacking background depth. Refine visuals to highlight key aspects for immediate comprehension. Communicate not just isolated facts but integrated narratives woven together into intuitive flow.

Impactful data stories incorporate fundamental elements:

- Spotlight metrics using the optimal visualization style - bars, lines or pie charts - to accent essential points

- Structure logical sequencing to walk audiences through incremental revelations

- Maintain topical coherence across narrative and imagery

- Incorporate interactive features for ongoing engagement

- Promote accessibility through clear designs optimized for comprehension

The simplicity yet intuitiveness of images allows broader groups to readily digest complex relationships. While spreadsheets conceal actionable intel, well-crafted charts and visual narratives speak volumes.

Data stories require straddling art and science across exploration and explanation. Blend analytical rigor with creative flair to produce accounts that inform perspectives and inspire change. Let visual narratives guide stakeholders toward sound, data-driven decisions.

Situations Where Data Storytelling Does or Doesn't Make Sense

Choosing the right data storytelling approach aligned to your goals and context is key for impact. Clarifying when these narrative techniques shine or falter across various scenarios provides helpful signposts. In this piece, I'll overview comparison guideposts and attribute spectra to aid your discernment process as you customize accounts for maximum resonance. My aim is equipping you with models to determine alignment between data story forms and intended communication outcomes.

Why Attributes Matter

Not all data storytelling applications effectively achieve objectives. Several key attributes distinguish optimal conditions from less suited contexts. Comparing goals and data inputs across spectrums like "exploratory vs explanatory" or "abstract vs concrete" allows appropriate calibration regarding usage of generalized reporting tactics or selective narrative customization.

While reporting has merits for broad information sharing, data stories thrive through conveying profound insights that compel action. Recognizing distinction nuances provides clarity when constructing narratives for maximum influence. Let's explore spectra as guides for discerning resonance.

Key Data Story Comparison Points

Five polar attributes offer helpful benchmarks:

Informative vs Insightful

Information has value for updating knowledge across wide contexts yet profound insights better sway decisions by drilling down on specific discoveries.

Exploratory vs Explanatory

Enabling audiences to independently interact with data can foster external analysis skills. However, employing narratives to simplify explanations around complex findings, interpretations or solutions boosts comprehension.

Abstract vs Concrete

Allowing flexible data interpretations enables diverse viewing angles but concrete specifics encourage alignment around targeted perspectives and actions.

Continuous vs Finite

Automated, ongoing reporting efficiently provides fresh metric updates while data storytelling extracts distinct snapshots to deeply examine before details shift.

Automated vs Curated

Technologies reliably funnel broad data at scale while human discernment during story curation spotlights deeper meaning.

The sweet spot for data narratives? Situations exhibiting concrete insights with clear implications that pass the "So What?" test of significance. For example, while showcasing the dipping conversion rates across South American markets informs sales leaders on macro-trends, spotlighting how a micro-targeted email series reversed the declining email open rates in Brazil within two weeks signals an optimization opportunity. This profound insight sparks immediate decisions.

Choose data story forms when concrete insights hold power for directing outcomes. Opt for broad reporting when transmitting generalized information without need for profound engagement. Recognizing when narratives can shine guides impact.

Application Guidance

Analyzing where your goals fall along these comparison spectra provides application guidance regarding data storytelling, reporting and alternative information delivery approaches. Not every situation warrants an intricate narrative format. However, when core insights emerge holding power for focusing attention and driving change, data stories bring them to life through contextualization and flow.

For sales operations professionals, as data complexity expands across systems, recognizing appropriate applications for storytelling techniques allows you to cut through noise to reach resonance. Let these models guide you in discerning when curated narratives will enhance communication effectiveness to produce data-informed decisions fueling organizational success!

4 Step Story Creation

Constructing compelling data narratives with the power to inform perspectives and motivate change requires navigating key phases in the insight curation process. From uncovering discoveries during exploration to explaining findings through framed storytelling, multiple models provide helpful signposts.

Here the attributes morph too between continuous, broad information sharing and finite, curated discovery explanation. The crucial moment comes in transitioning from raw information to framed patterns and ultimately contextualized findings. Recognizing when to utilize generalized reporting, storyframing exploration or selective data storytelling is key to communication effectiveness.

The Dual Analysis and Storytelling Journey

An informative continuum displays the fluid relationship between data storytelling and other reporting approaches. This spectrum provides helpful context on when and how to activate different formats.

On one far end sits automated metric reporting – reliably channeling information without nuanced human refinement. Mid-spectrum lies exploratory storyframing to unearth insightful measures and dimensions. At the farthest point resides contextualized data storytelling itself – weaving together narrative elements and visuals that accentuate hand-picked insights warranting spotlight to compel choices.

The differentiators morph too as we traverse from broad recurring feeds toward specific curated accounts. The art comes in discerning when raw metrics transform from indistinct figures into framed patterns and ultimately profound findings ready for insightful narratives.

During exploratory storyframing, we focus on playing data detective – combing noise to discover gems while defining categories and measures that show initial significance. Think wide investigation chasing sparks.

Yet at times, an excavated insight merits elevating beyond the raw visuals used while exploring. These profound findings require tailored explanatory narratives – honing storylines and graphics to underscore implications prompting action. Here we adopt the data storyteller mantle to transform metrics into meaning.

Recognizing when to shift gears from framing to weaving data into purposeful narratives strikes an optimal balance between exploration and explanation that makes communication compelling.

Data Story Creation Process

Data storytelling takes metrics beyond isolated reporting to compelling narratives that catalyze change. When crafted skillfully, quantitative insights transform into qualitative meaning that compels belief, informs perspectives and guides outcomes.

Although narrative formats vary, four key steps fuel impactful data story construction:

1. Spotlight Your Eureka Finding

2. Build Context and Spark Engagement

3. Substantiate Through Intentional Flow

4. Guide Action

While additional intricacies abound, this reliable four-step blueprint builds solid data story foundations aligned to audience goals. Let's explore best practices within each phase to put insights into motion.

Step 1: Spotlight Your Eureka Finding

Defining the singular, spotlight-worthy nugget is pivotal. Consider why this headline insight passes the "so what?" test relevantly and meaningfully given audience interests and organizational objectives using precise language. This data revelation will steer the overall narrative arc, so launch storyboarding with clarity on your destination finding to imbue purpose.

For example, describe implications succinctly using concrete terminology. Quantify the insight's impact on critical metrics – projected cost savings, revenue expansion, service level improvements. Attach a monetary value. Precision provides proof of concept and grounds narratives for business audiences fixated on returns.

A well-defined eureka insight anchors data stories with poignancy that sharpens audience engagement. Spend time crystallizing why this headline deserves a compelling, curated narrative elevating intimate details otherwise lost amid wider reporting noise.

Step 2: Build Context and Spark Engagement

Balancing orientation and captivation, introduce key concepts then craft an intriguing "hook" observation that entices curiosity and primes audiences to appreciate upcoming storylines traced by your substantive metrics.

Determine baseline knowledge needs then efficiently build context so groups readily grasp findings. Outline histories, challenges addressed or ineffective past tactics as appropriate without delving deeper than required. The purpose here is micro not macro.

With backgrounds established, pose a compelling puzzle the data story resolves - reference familiar leadership frustrations, known capability gaps. This dual move to orient and intrigue audiences prepares them for illuminated eureka moments in the narrative ascent ahead.

Step 3: Curate Substantiating Flows

The heartbeat of engaging data stories is the strategic selection and sequence of quantified evidence that compounds listener comprehension of featured takeaways. Diligent curation separates fragmented reporting from connected accounts that compel belief.

Be highly selective in showcasing only the most relevant supporting metrics needed to reinforce core findings. Ensure each insight unveiled across deliberate sequencing implicitly edges audiences closer toward climatic revelations without tangents that derail momentum. Concision and coherence rule; clutter obscures.

Additionally, pay close attention to logical flow bridges smoothly transitioning audiences from one data point to the next. Do revelations unfold in an intuitive path mirroring thought progression? Identify and address gaps disrupting seamless connections tying metrics together into an anticipatory arc headed directly toward central money-saving, revenue-enabling or customer-serving approaches worthy of spotlighting.

Step 4: Guide Action

Reach partial impact if audiences lack direction to apply featured insights post-narrative. Stakeholders inspired yet execution-unclear cannot activate findings to drive outcomes. Losing momentum devastates after achieving initial comprehension.

So conclusively, underscore operational implications, facilitate outstanding question discussions, and explicitly define decisions or directions sparked by central insights. Provide implementation guidance. Recommend ideal next phases post-analysis. Welcome continued dialogue to further buy-in for data-inspired trajectories.

Balancing exploratory details with pragmatic explanations ultimately empowers perspectives and catalyzes change. Masterfully navigating key phases - revelation, substantiation and guided activation - allows artfully contextualized metrics to direct decision pathways toward better organizational futures through prompt action.

Key Takeaways

- Debunk assumptions that all data visuals tell stories or that more metrics strengthen narratives - curation and flow matter more.

- Build in explanatory focus to clarify reasons behind data patterns, along with deliberate sequencing that progressively unveils insights.

- Balance quantitative foundations with engaging qualitative elements like settings and characters that emotionally connect.

- Traverse from exploration where visuals uncover insights to explanation where refined graphics and narrative context simplify findings.

- Recognize when concrete insights warrant elevating metrics into full data stories versus just informing through reporting.

- Follow a 4-step process to spotlight eureka findings, build anticipatory context, substantiate via intentional flow and catalyze change through implications.

Chapter 7
Communicating Insights Through Data-Driven Storytelling

D ata-driven storytelling is a key skill for sales operations managers to effectively translate analytics into informed decisions and actions. This chapter explores creating visual data narratives, understanding diverse audience needs, and utilizing techniques to build compelling, resonant tales. Defining strategic messages and goals lets sales operations craft stories that connect across stakeholder groups, promoting engagement and desired behaviors.

Alexander Group research highlights a growing gap between what sales organizations require and what sales operations can deliver. More data than ever is available, but sales needs help transforming disjointed reports and spreadsheets into meaningful insights that spark incremental growth. Sales operations play a crucial role in extracting essential meaning from data and guiding practical application to improve results.

Understanding Your Audience for Maximum Impact

Appreciating diverse viewpoints is vital for data storytelling that compels belief and action. Sales operations must customize messaging for distinct internal groups - frontline reps, regional managers, executives - rather than taking a one-size-fits-all reporting approach. Each audience has different interests, needs and responsibilities driving the metrics and next steps they prioritize. Failure to recognize these core perspective differences results in generic communication missing the mark across the board.

For example, reps may fixate on lead volume, conversion rates and win probability forecasts most related to their quota chase. Regional managers could prioritize broader pipeline health, deal progression pace and historical close rate consistency to guide frontline coaching. Executives tend to concentrate on market share, revenue expansion and external benchmarking indicators relevant to shareholders.

Without customization, disjointed datasets overwhelm and distract each group rather than clarifying situational significance. The key is to identify the specific metrics, goals and pain points most critical to each audience.

Then sales operations can spotlight insights explaining achievement challenges for reps, reveal coaching opportunities for managers to raise conversion rates, and convey strategic revelations on market trajectory for leadership planning. Reps need visibility into behaviors and skill gaps explaining performance contrasts so they can self-correct. Managers require access into regional progression patterns and coaching needs to guide their teams' growth. Executives want market share and revenue forecasts to inform high-level decisions.

Matching communication channels to audiences also boosts retention and application. Email newsletters often overflow inboxes without grabbing attention. However, interactive peer benchmarking dashboards can redirect rep focus towards tangible self-improvement during quota chases. Scheduled digital briefings with executives using customized scorecards may reveal crucial trends that spur strategy adjustments.

The key is grasping varied perspectives across sales organizations in order to craft data stories that resonate through relevance enhancement. The payoff comes through unification around aligned objectives and elevation of enterprise data fluency.

Defining Strategic Messages and Objectives

Clearly articulating key narratives and intentions ensures data insights connect to overarching business goals. Sales operations must align analytics to strategy, clarify purpose, assess relevance, communicate consistently and build in adaptivity.

Strategic Alignment

Data stories should directly support overall business direction to drive decisions and actions that spur targeted growth outcomes. Misaligned insights fail on relevance. For example, short-term focused sales analytics will lack context for leaders weighing longer-horizon product investments and market positioning goals 5+ years out.

Leaders balancing future ambitions and immediate returns need projections matched to their strategic planning timeframes. Therefore, sales operations should actively consult executive priorities and intelligence requirements as a prerequisite for effective quantification through data narratives. Use collaborative sessions to craft supporting metrics purposefully designed to fill strategy knowledge gaps - not just report available data disjointed from planning needs. Explicitly connect revelations to crucial trade-off choices influencing leadership's growth objectives.

Clarity of Purpose

Additionally, plainly state upfront the exact purpose and desired response intended from each reporting item. Articulate how insights aim to shift awareness, inform resource trade-offs, improve reliability or address other precise decision constraints faced by target audience members based on their realm of control and priorities. Vary contextual framing and urgency based on each group's functional responsibilities. Close with clear data-driven calls to action for operational changes, strategy recommendations or budget reallocations. Purpose clarity ensures facts spark decisions.

Ensuring Ongoing Relevance

Regularly revalidate reporting resonance amidst evolving landscapes to combat declining relevance. Create nimble reporting capabilities through adjustable modular components that allow rapid reorientation when situational dynamics shift assumptions. Input ongoing audience feedback to guide effectiveness improvements. Above all, continually assess and confirm surfaced insights directly address current decision constraints and uncertainties faced by leadership.

Achieving maximum influence requires tight strategy alignment, plain purpose communication, and resilience to change through continual relevance checks. The outcome is collectively embraced insights that accelerate advancement.

Techniques for Engaging Data Narratives

Employing specific techniques breathes impact and conviction into data communications. Sales operations should structure insights as intriguing narratives, establish emotional connections, provide context, curate relevant metrics and creatively visualize revelations to compel understanding and action.

Have a Story Framework

Structure data insights as intriguing narratives like great literature – with a beginning, middle and end – to fully capture audience attention. Introduce leadership's current dilemma. Develop rising complexity by highlighting conflicting datapoints that deepen uncertainty. Then resolve tension by contextualizing revelations, stating conclusions and outlining data-driven actions to overcome obstacles. This arc motivates embracing analytics-guided imperatives in a way scattered facts cannot.

Making Emotional Connections

Also incorporate relatable human perspectives linking statistics to intrinsic motivations data alone cannot inspire. Profile customer personas who share values with sales teams to deepen loyalty commitments despite tempting competitor offers. Localize overseas manufacturing realities through photo journeys affirming the need for quality interventions that value community stewardship. Make abstract economic indicators relatable by contrasting against previous boom-and-bust cycles that altered careers of current leaders. Help audiences personally connect with revelations to spark advocacy.

Providing Explanatory Context

Equally important is explanatory backstory answering the "why does this matter" question lurking behind metrics. Frame sales declines amid corresponding currency shifts diminishing local buying power to guide appropriate executive response. Clarify website analytics by first explaining intended goals of latest publicity campaigns.

Constantly anchor metrics in explanatory context preempting false assumptions around causality and significance before misguided actions undermine strategies.

Curating Focused Data Selections

Additionally, carefully curate reports to exclusively showcase metrics directly empowering clarity and appropriate actions for each audience. Eliminate tangential indicators confusing teams struggling to balance complex interdependent decisions amid overflowing inboxes. Restraint helps focus attention with purposeful intent instead of accurate but disjointed data.

Data narratives crafted through deliberate frameworks, emotional connections, contextual backstories and curated details better inspire belief and understanding required for outcomes alignment. Creative messaging propels teams beyond confusion.

Key Takeaways

- Customize messaging and medium for different internal audiences like frontline reps, managers and executives based on their distinct interests and responsibilities.

- Align data stories directly to overarching business goals and strategy timeframes. Articulate precise purpose and desired responses.

- Continually revalidate reporting resonance amid changing landscapes to ensure ongoing relevance.

- Make emotional connections and provide context so metrics relate on a personal level to intrinsically motivate audiences.

- Structure revealing metrics as intriguing narratives with framework arcs building tension and resolving through data-guided actions.

- Carefully curate reports to focus insights exclusively on the most empowering details for each audience to compel clarity and alignment.

Chapter 8

Aligning Data Visualization with Business Goals

A ligning data visualization with business goals is a critical yet often overlooked aspect of effective sales operations management. Without clear alignment, data visualizations fail to convey relevant insights, inform strategic decisions, and inspire stakeholder action. This article explores best practices for tying visualization closely to overarching objectives. First, we discuss identifying key performance indicators, mapping them to goals, and defining crucial sales metrics. Next, we outline principles for creating insightful, actionable reports and dashboards catered to diverse internal audiences. Proper alignment of visuals empowers organizations to communicate strategy, support data-driven choices, and unlock the motivational potential of information.

Mapping KPIs to Business Goals

Mapping key performance indicators (KPIs) to business goals ensures visualizations contribute meaningfully to objectives rather than operating in a vacuum. It facilitates conveying relevant messages, tracking progress, and revealing actionable insights tailored to strategic priorities. Approaching this alignment deliberately and collaboratively leads to maximum organizational value.

You should start by clearly identifying and articulating primary business goals across departments. Common objectives include increasing revenue by a certain percentage yearly, boosting customer lifetime value, reducing customer churn rate, shortening sales cycles, expanding market share in key segments, improving brand awareness and perception, decreasing cost per acquisition or lead, and lifting customer satisfaction or Net Promoter Score.

With goals formalized, assess how each selected KPI directly relates to and impacts them. Revenue maps clearly to a revenue growth objective. Customer lifetime value ties to boosting retention and share of wallet. Brand awareness links with perception and market expansion aims. Make sure to consider leading and lagging indicators that either predict or reflect goal progress. Leading KPIs like sales pipeline health anticipate future revenue. Lagging KPIs like closed deals evaluate past performance.

Additionally, contemplate the strategic influence of KPIs on long-term success. Metrics focused on immediate results or narrow departments often lack strategic perspective. For example, the number of sales calls measures activity but not effectiveness. Assess indicators on alignment with customer-centricity, future scalability, and other strategic priorities.

With the backdrop of goals, regularly review and update mapping to accommodate evolving business priorities. Quarterly or annual refreshes provide cadence while retaining flexibility to pivot based on trends, competitive forces, technology shifts, economic fluctuations, and other external factors.

Lastly, clearly communicate the relationship between KPIs and business objectives across the organization. Consistent understanding aligns behaviors and decision-making to strategy. Transparency also increases context for metrics, inspiring action beyond superficial numbers.

Defining Sales Metrics

Defining well-rounded sales metrics involves identifying indicators that collectively contribute to achieving business goals. First, adopt a holistic approach spanning the entire sales process, not just isolated aspects. Core metric categories often include volume of qualified leads, sales calls, opportunities and pipeline creation, conversion rates by stage, closed and lost deals, customer retention and expansion, profit margins, customer lifetime value, and market share relative to addressable opportunity.

Additionally, involve key cross-functional stakeholders in metric definition rather than unilaterally deciding in a vacuum. Sales reps offer frontline perspective on leading indicators of success and adoption of defined measures. Sales operations and information technology validate feasibility of systematic tracking and reporting. Finance applies profitability lens and models monetization. Marketing weighs early-funnel generation. Executives safeguard alignment to company strategy. Collectively addressing diverse viewpoints results in balanced, pragmatic metrics.

A balanced scorecard framework provides helpful guidance ensuring a well-rounded perspective on sales achievement. It examines financial outlook through margins, profitability, lifetime customer value, and similar monetary gauges. Customer viewpoint tracks satisfaction, churn risks, expansion results, and relationship growth through net promoter and satisfaction scores. Internal process effectiveness evaluates sales processes, velocity, and operational efficiency. Finally, learning and growth monitors talent development, capability-building, and other human capital facets. Together these lenses construct holistic sales health measurement.

Additionally, incorporate both quantitative performance metrics around revenue as well as qualitative metrics around customer experience and brand integrity. Quantitative KPIs enable objective assessments and benchmarks. But qualitative indicators reveal nuanced sales effectiveness not captured purely by numbers.

Strategically aligning data visualization empowers deriving meaning, informing decisions, and inspiring action tailored to business goals. Deliberately mapping KPIs to objectives and defining comprehensive sales success metrics provides the foundation for visuals to communicate insights rather than data alone. Establishing this directional linkage between measures and goals allows reports and dashboards to unlock the true motivational and analytical potential of data. With these best practices, analytics transitions from isolated numbers to visualized narratives conveying progress towards strategic priorities throughout the organization. The ability to inform, inspire and align through data represents a pivotal driver of competitive advantage and sales achievement.

Best Practices for Sales Reporting

Sales reporting provides invaluable visibility into the health and performance of revenue-driving activities. To realize the full strategic potential of reports, organizations must move beyond static documents to dynamic visualizations enabling real-time monitoring, intuitive consumption and proactive interventions. This article outlines techniques for creating insightful dashboards, designing visually compelling layouts, and leveraging automation to drive sales excellence through data.

Creating Insightful Dashboards

Dashboards play a pivotal role in condensing metric overload into accessible visual snapshots to inform decisions. Effective sales dashboards prominently feature the most critical KPIs for immediate attention from users. Leading indicators of performance such as net new sales pipeline creation, opportunity conversion rates by stage, and sales activity levels equip teams to gauge progress proactively instead of awaiting lagging reports.

Additionally, real-time or near real-time data updates prevent outdated information from clouding perspectives. Manual refresh workflows for dashboards often result in versions rapidly decaying into obsolescence as new data emerges. Automating pipelines to feed visualizations current information should become a baseline expectation.

While highlighting the vital few metrics, also allow users to customize displays to fit specific informational needs. Personalization fosters richer contexts for interpreting data based on roles and priorities. Sales leaders may focus more on forecast accuracy, pipeline health funnels, and productivity metrics while account managers analyze territory opportunities and individual deal progression.

Enable this tailored functionality while also maintaining consistency in fundamental visualizations like core KPI Waterfalls, geographic performance heatmaps, and deal stage conversion funnels. Standardizing platforms, views, and metrics across groups improves unified understanding.

Additionally, guarantee accessibility across devices with mobile-optimized designs. Reps in the field lose crucial decision support capabilities if dashboards only function on desktop monitors. Responsiveness bolsters capabilities to monitor dynamically updated dashboards from anywhere.

Finally, provide thorough training on navigating dashboards while also promoting broader accessibility to data. Sales teams gain little from polished visuals without fluency in extracting and applying insights. And limiting viewing rights to senior leadership deprives frontline professionals of the visibility needed to adjust tactical activities. Dashboard adoption and data literacy upskilling enable ROI realization.

Monitoring KPIs in Real Time

The potential of dashboards remains unfulfilled without real-time monitoring of KPIs to trigger proactive interventions. Manual inspection of lagging reports results in delayed response. Automating monitoring through live dashboards, alert systems, and flexible review processes powers dynamic sales management.

Establish automated reporting systems to continuously collect and visualize updated KPI data, avoiding lags from batched reporting. Building systematic pipelines eliminates reliance on individual efforts to prepare reports. And instead of defaulting to lengthy quarterly or annual reviews, automate visualization of key metrics on daily, weekly or monthly cycles fitting their volatility.

Additionally, configure alert systems to notify stakeholders immediately when predefined performance thresholds breached. Sales managers receive alerts when the sales qualified opportunity conversion rate dips below 80 percent or the SQL to SAL lead throughput slows. Responding rapidly limits deterioration of metrics before the next scheduled dashboard update.

Set alert triggers and monitoring cycles specific to each KPI based on criticality and natural fluctuation patterns. Watch volatile indicators like net new pipeline creation daily while monitoring more stable metrics like average deal size quarterly. Adapt review periodicity and alerts to the sales process context.

Finally, regularly review the effectiveness of monitoring mechanisms for continuous improvement. Assess whether alert triggers and cycles reveal changes early enough for successful intervention or need adjustment. Continue honing automation and practices as the business evolves.

Principles for Intuitive Analysis

The intuitive design of visualizations proves vital for seamless consumption by diverse sales stakeholders. Cluttered displays packed densely with metrics hamper ability to quickly spot insights. Applying key principles enhances intuitive analysis to unlock value.

First, thoughtfully structure dashboards and reports to establish clear visual hierarchy and flow. Lead viewers through prioritized content in order of importance. Group related metrics into clear sections to form narrative rather than randomly scattering individual charts. Introduce overarching Performance Summary views before drilling down into nuanced analyses like Conversion Funnels, Activity Trends, and Geographic Breakdowns. Guide consumption deliberately.

Additionally, maintain consistent branding elements across visualizations like logos, fonts, color schemes and iconography. A cohesive visual identity strings together charts into a professional, unified presentation easier to quickly parse. Design harmony establishes trust and authority.

Speaking of color, wield it purposefully to accent, highlight patterns, denote differences and communicate meaning. Use sparingly and thoughtfully direct attention, establish connections and encode status at a glance through intuitive color coding. For example, apply red hues to represent shortfall metrics and green hues for areas exceeding goals.

Furthermore, actively utilize whitespace and negative space to prevent dense, cluttered designs. Apply white space between logical sections and frame individual charts. Let backgrounds breathe around key numbers and snippets pulled out. Uncluttered designs prove more consumable, memorable and instantly scannable for time-pressed sales professionals.

Finally, continually conduct user testing with target stakeholders to refine designs and layouts based on how they actually interpret and utilize reports. Their feedback oft uncovers gaps between intended and actual functionality. Iterate to maximize intuitive analysis.

Implementing dynamic, automated sales reporting transforms static data documents into intuitive visual tools empowering real-time interventions. Strategically highlighting KPIs on mobile-accessible dashboards provides instant performance visibility. Automating monitoring via sophisticated alert systems enables rapid response to fluctuations. And applying design principles catalyzes seamless consumption by the full range of sales professionals. Unlocking these capabilities accelerates data-driven decision making and excellence through analytics.

Customizing Visualizations for Different Stakeholders

Data visualizations lose impact and usefulness when generically designed without the specific needs of target stakeholder groups in mind. Customizing reporting and dashboards to the preferences and responsibilities of viewing audiences drives adoption and impact. This article explores best practices for tailoring designs and interactivity to sales teams, managers and executives. We discuss understanding varying needs, employing adaptable templates, guiding customization, upholding design principles, and balancing interactive dynamism with static simplicity. Thoughtful personalization empowers converting raw data into meaningful insights.

Understanding Needs of Sales Stakeholders

The first step in effective customization involves gaining an intimate understanding of the distinct perspectives and requirements for each stakeholder group. Frontline sales representatives focus more on their individual pipeline health, territory opportunities and activity metrics to guide tactical prioritization. Sales managers take a broader view tracking team performance across multiple indicators like total pipeline value, stage conversion rates, forecast accuracy, and closed deal velocity. Executives monitor primarily strategic KPIs including revenue growth, customer acquisition costs, brand sentiment shifts and market share to inform high-level positioning.

These divergent needs shape dashboard designs. Sales reps may value reports with granular opportunity details, personalized activity goals, comparison to peers and contest leaderboards. Managers prioritize consolidated team views highlighting critical conversion funnel stages, bottlenecks, recurring lost reasons and quarterly projections. Executives prefer summaries of revenue backlogs, customer segmentation penetration, retention risks and market benchmarks. Understand nuanced requirements through stakeholder interviews and job shadowing before designing.

Adaptable and Collaborative Customization

With perspective on distinct needs, create adaptable reporting system architectures and templates flexible enough for personalization without fully manual recreations for every viewer. Build re-usable components like performance cards, KPI visualizations, filtering mechanics, color palettes and chart types. Construct layout templates catering to different focuses with sections for territory/team/market analyses, productivity indicators, conversion views and projection forecasting.

Then enable collaborative customization engaging stakeholders, not just analysts unilateral decisions. Provide user interfaces for sales reps to showcase key opportunity or activity metrics preferentially. Let managers dictate priority KPIs and team grouping. Involve executives in high-level dashboard structuring showcasing strategic commercial, customer and competitive intelligence. Capturing diverse viewpoints through co-creation prevents narrow assumptions bisecting usefulness. Guide audiences in applying customization while upholding governance standards.

Additionally, sustain adaptability for changing internal mobility and external conditions. Promote modular components to fluidly reorganize as responsibilities evolve. Maintain flexibility allowing new metrics and dimensions to address market fluctuations. No dashboard design stands statically forever. Keep iterating.

Principles for Intuitive Design

While empowering tailored reporting for each audience, also uphold fundamental design principles promoting intuitive navigation, visual coherence and quick insight derivation.

First, optimize the layout hierarchy directing focus and flow intuitively for viewers. Structure dashboards through a clear information architecture guiding analysis logically from summarized Scorecards to specific Performance Drivers, Granular Breakdowns only then detailed backing Data Tables. Guide viewing deliberately through progressive disclosure. Also create logical groupings between related metrics depicting conversion stages, process phases or customer lifecycle.

Furthermore, maintain consistent visual themes across charts through coordinated palettes, typography, iconography and styling. Consistent branding strings together diverse dashboards into a professional, governing style. But then allow flexibility within those constraints.

Additionally, apply principles of highlighting, contrast and whitespace management to draw attention appropriately based on context. Leverage highlighting judiciously to accentuate priority KPIs or alerts based on user needs. Manipulate whitespace to direct focus and improve chart comprehension. Promote scanning for time-constrained executives.

Balancing Interactive and Static Visuals

The optimal balance between dynamic, interactive dashboarding and static visualization reporting depends significantly on the sales role, required usage cadence and proficiency of consumers. Generally, interactive dashboards enable more rapid, ad hoc analysis for scenarios requiring frequent visibility by technically adept users into latest data. Static reports serve lightweight information delivery needs through straightforward charts focused on delivering key snapshots quickly.

Evaluate interactivity against flexibility requirements for each audience. Reps may drill dynamically into territory details. Managers can filter team groupings interactively during weekly reviews. Executives often require only high-level summaries updated monthly not meriting full dynamism. In addition, guide less proficient dashboard navigators through training and support improving their self-service. Blend both approaches for balance.

Strategically customizing visualizations to address the unique priorities of each sales stakeholder group improves adoption and impact of data. Gaining intimate understanding of their needs, wants and perspectives fuels tailored designs over one-size-fits-all. Collaborating on flexible templates adhering to design principles grounds effective personalization. And blending interactivity with targeted static delivery caters to use cases. Thoughtful customization unlocks relevance and utility.

Key Takeaways

- Map key performance indicators directly to overarching business objectives to ensure relevance and convey strategic progress.

- Involve cross-functional input in sales metric definition for balance across process stages and perspectives. Adopt a scorecard approach.

- Create insightful dashboards prominently featuring the most crucial leading indicators, updated continuously in real time.

- Allow dashboard customization while upholding standardized structures and visual themes for consistency. Ensure mobile optimization.

- Automate monitoring and alerts tied to sale KPI thresholds to trigger rapid, proactive interventions when fluctuations occur.

- Apply design principles like hierarchy, highlighting, whitespace management and branding coherence for intuitive analysis.

- Customize reporting across stakeholder groups based on their distinct needs and responsibilities to boost relevance and adoption.

Chapter 9
Data-Driven Decision-Making

A s a sales operations professional, you know first-hand that the fast-paced and rapidly evolving sales environment leaves little room for guesswork, assumptions, or operating based just on intuition. To drive performance, identify issues early, and capitalize on new opportunities, sales leaders must cultivate widespread data fluency across their teams and organizations. Relying on hard, empirical data to inform decisions provides fact-based confidence to guide strategies and optimize processes amidst constant change. With the right analytical infrastructure, adoption of data-driven practices at all levels, and skills development, organizations can elevate decisions through data - transforming reactive guesswork into confident, proactive action.

Recognizing Patterns in Data

The foundation of data-driven decision making lies in recognizing meaningful patterns across metrics instead of assessing each KPI in isolation. It means synthesizing indicators collectively to reveal crucial correlations, performance drivers, and outlier impacts that would otherwise go unseen. Sales managers who can interpret integrated data narratives - not just analyze numerical tables - gain an invaluable perspective.

Let's consider an example to illustrate this point. Say you start noticing declining lead-to-opportunity conversion rates, but pipeline health also shrinking at the same time. Instead of jumping to vague external explanations, view conversion rates alongside sales activity levels and pipeline velocity metrics. The integrated data story may surface clear links between dropping activity levels and shrinking pipeline, which in turn squeeze conversions. Identifying these causal chains between KPIs means you can address the root issue rather than applying band-aids down the line.

The takeaway? Encourage your teams to connect the patterns across metrics instead of assessing each discretely. Guide them to recognize chains, correlations, and outlier impacts. Doing so transforms scattered data points into an insightful narrative that leads to confident decisions.

Incorporating Real-Time Data

In the world of sales operations, decision cycles move fast, so you cannot always wait for delayed static reporting to guide choices. This makes leveraging real-time visibility critical. Dynamic data on emerging performance issues allows for rapid response instead of lengthy retrospective analysis on past trends.

Here is my recommendation - build data infrastructure with automated dashboards that pipes the latest information to you and your teams. Set up thresholds that trigger alerts when key metrics fall outside an acceptable range. This means sales ops leaders can take quick corrective action at the first signs of underperformance instead of after major dips. Getting ahead of issues preserves revenue and relationships.

Beyond infrastructure, promote a culture focused on monitoring real-time indicators at micro and macro levels - not just rearview reporting. Advance tools are useless if teams don't continually track emerging data stories. So incentivize habits for regularly checking dynamic visibility tools and immediately addressing deviations. This muscle memory prepares staff to catch problems proactively, making decisive moves as market needs and realities shift.

Encouraging Transparent Data Dialogues

Driving adoption of data-based decisions also requires open, non-judgemental data dialogues across teams. This means establishing a collaborative culture that encourages curiosity about performance variations, rational questioning of root causes, and transparency about uncertainties or knowledge gaps.

Frame structured data discussions for participants to deliberately separate human/behavioral factors from underlying process drivers behind the numbers. Guide teams to openly consider multiple interpretations, air uncertainties, and settle on fact-based actions - not gut reactions or assumptions. Reward critical thinking and evidence-based exchange.

You'll often spot gaps in data comprehension this way so you can target relevant skill building. And facilitating non-judgmental data transparency breaks stigmas that block sharing. Over time these collaborative sessions will build 'data-driven muscle memory' for independent decisions later.

Advancing Analytical Proficiency

Finally, help your sales operations teams advance their proficiency in data analytics beyond basic skill sets. Level up their capabilities to move from simple reporting into specialized analysis like statistical models, predictive metrics, contribution weighting, correlation mapping and smart visualizations. This injects powerful and nuanced insights directly into field decision sequences while building analytical prowess across the org.

Without advancing data skills, sales teams tend to default to aged assumptions, past experiences, or intuition when choices arise. But mastering real-time data tactics, structured transparency practices, and advanced analysis methods unlocks pervasive, confident and quick data-driven decisions - even as markets and priorities shift.

Bridging Insight and Action

Deriving pivotal insights without the capability to compel collective conviction and change limits analytical impact to personal enlightenment. Organizations often overlook the crucial final mile separating revelation from revolution – strategic communication transforming observation into unified movement. This chapter explores the complex human dynamics, biases and burdens blocking receptivity, undermining validity and impeding action even upon sound insights. We then discuss philosophies and mechanisms for breakthrough messaging that inform, inspire and activate audiences. With compelling narrative and empowering visuals, data transcends paralysis to become an instrument for influence and change.

Understanding the People Dimension

Logical data-based insights crash against cognitive obstacles without delicately addressing the human factors gating acceptance especially disruptive truths. Whether an internal analyst or external industry observer, the first challenge involves establishing source credibility and rapport with audiences often inherently skeptical of conclusions conflicting with existing perspectives. Rather than bombard with facts, first navigate the landmine of perceived positioning either as a detached outsider lacking internal context or a privileged insider oblivious to ground realities. Customize framing based on the relationship backdrop even presenting the same empirical insight.

Furthermore, recognize analysis rarely precipitates change through independent action but rather collective conviction across networks of colleagues, subordinates and superiors. Evaluate the power dynamics and cultural nuances surrounding target stakeholders based on hierarchy, function and history. Customize navigational strategies for facts potentially conflicting with management stances based on organizational maturity to handle inconvenient truths. The wise analyst targets allies likely to endorse findings instead of barriers likely to suppress them.

Overcoming Communication Oversight

Another pitfall lies in assumption that analytical validity alone ensures adoption, forgetting communication itself as a capability to build explicitly. Statistical significance, insightful correlations and even elegantly modeled projections may still fail to permeate organizational obstruction if simply dumped in raw technical form bereft of digestible packaging and emotional punch. Just as formulating the research question and hypotheses requires deliberation before commencing data gathering, strategize presentation, positioning and persuasion upfront alongside analytical design. Build narrative structure, simplifying metaphors and memorable visuals in parallel to analysis. Treat communication as integral to process not an afterthought.

The first step in this orientation flip involves recognizing the non-linear journey from observations to outcomes. Insights, even if embraced, rarely directly prompt change but rather trigger cyclical sequences of comprehension, consultation, objection resolution and confidence building essential for securing approval. Allow time and repeat messaging for organizational digestion across multiple exposures. Furthermore, inject two-way engagement through dialogue to expose mental models and address doubts. Communication oversight severely hinders traction for even the soundest conclusions.

Conquering Resistance through Stories

People inherently resist changing established workflows, philosophies and beliefs by default lacking an emotionally compelling catalyst strong enough to overwhelm inherent inertia bias. Both those expected to implement insights and influencers advocating them internally encounter skepticism and demands for justification especially for conclusions contradicting legacy perspectives. Arm insights with preemptive inoculation against predictable doubts by immersing recommendations within resonating storytelling.

For example, personalized anecdotes of specific customers helped by optimizations build intrinsic motivation. Weave data-backed insights into an overarching growth narrative people wish to write themselves into not forced to accept. Highlight early adopters already benefitting. Outline how small tests stayed true to values while improving performance before asking for scale commitment. Appeal first to hearts, then to heads before hands.

Stories also powerfully tackle resistance by portraying the cost of clinging to familiarity. Case studies of peers disrupted after dismissing early warning signs caution against paralytic prudence. If large enough companies can fall suddenly, no position remains inherently secure without continuous agility. Inject a spirit of healthy, hunger through success stories balanced with failure warnings.

Finally, continuous reinforcement through multi-channel drip campaigns sustains momentum compensating our tendency to forget inconvenient messages. Dose insights across meetings, emails, posters and events until organizational bloodstream until it finally tips culture.

Informing to Influencing Shift

The pivot from purely informing stakeholders to actively influencing them hinges on transcending detached data delivery through passionate exchange. Resist hiding behind charts slavishly presenting numbers without perspective as though neutrality equals objectivity. Dry statistics alone rarely rally people to difficult action even when accurately signaling necessity simply because they fail to signal urgency. Augment raw figures with vivid framing elucidating meaning and implications tailored to the audience. Frame data within values.

For example, inject tangible human impacts behind retention rates, not just mathematical extrapolations. Make abstract percentages feel visceral through stories conveying how product flaws undermine customer trust or delays erode loyalty daily. Quantify pain points through money or time lost. Vividly show how insights directly address voiced frustrations from the field. This reality framing erodes excuses to ignore insights by linking directly to identifiable individual consequences from inaction.

Additionally, wield the power of aspiration alongside apprehension. Balance warning signs with a roadmap for results if recommendations get implemented. Contrast the reality of problems with the potential upside if corrected early before deteriorated further. Inspire belief in a more profitable, harmonious future state achievable through data-driven decisiveness. Outline growth trajectories across revenue, customer satisfaction and innovation metrics from acting today with Case Studies proving concepts elsewhere. Positive potential acts as the carrot drawing stakeholders forward from fear-inducing sticks.

What is an Actionable Insight?

Leaders today face information overload and churning out reports and discovering statistical relationships means little if the insights uncovered don't spark action towards positive change. Within ever growing data, the crucial task lies in distinguishing truly meaningful signals from inconsequential noise.

Cultivating Relevance and Value

For analytics to resonate rather than simply take up mental space, findings must connect to your stakeholders' core frustrations, initiatives, or priorities. Insights divorced from the operational context fall flat, lacking intrinsic motivation for adoption. People inherently orient attention towards progress and pain points in their reality.

So take time to quantify how your revelations directly tie to expressed challenges your audiences face or ambitions they hold. What burning priorities or goals do your suggestions address? Where will proposed interventions alleviate anxieties or roadblocks? Anchoring insights in relatable contexts is powerful.

Furthermore, accentuate the tangible monetary value or savings possible behind any actions highlighted by analytics. Transform abstract statistical relationships into financial impetus like potential profit increases, cost reductions, risk mitigations or competitive advantages conveyed. For example, conveying precisely how much lost revenue is recoverable, how much profit is protectable, or how much market share is defensible shapes persuasive business cases your leadership can envision. Contrast implementation costs against sizable upside. Position insights as value catalysts. Combining relatability and value elevates engagement while lowering adoption barriers substantially.

Relevant insights lose impact if people are unclear on feasible responses within their control. Vague strategic plans frustrate. Instead, offer customized, step-by-step guidance. Where possible, break down analytic findings into actionable game plans. Outline specific options. Guide prioritization based on weighing effort against potential impact. Provide templates and tools to smooth the path from insight to action. Cover basics like owners, timelines, resource needs and success metrics.

Package recommendations in digestible steps to prevent initiatives stalling due to confusion on first moves. Tailor responses across functions, seniority levels and skill sets. People adopt insights more readily when advice speaks directly to their area. Emphasize their ability to activate findings through organizational change management.

Anchoring Impact with Context

Also quantitatively anchor insights to projected outcomes. Setting ambitious yet realistic forecasts underscores the business imperative while establishing informed expectations.

Arm leaders especially with contextual benchmarks for monitoring progress. These may involve historical comparisons, industry standards, previous iterations of related initiatives, and other key performance yardsticks.

For example, conveying that a 10% subscriber conversion lift historically increased deal values by 7% grounds recommendations with precedent. Frameworks quantifying addressable opportunities, risk reductions and profit potentials related to actions also compel engagement by delineating milestones.

Empowering Sales Operations with Actionable Insights

Simply unleashing torrents of data across a sales organization will fail to yield better decisions or performance without the advancement of analytical capabilities of the organization. As such, leaders must strategically increase both accessible visibility into relevant insights as well as internal proficiency in distilling findings into executable strategies, guided by overarching objectives. Empowered sales operations managers serve as the lynchpin bridging systemized data flows with human-centered uplift driving sustained competitive advantage.

Empowering sales operations requires a multi-dimensional approach spanning expanding access, uplifting strategy, honing acuity and sustaining systems scaling with market dynamism. Insights left unattended erode into wasted signals. Leadership must deliberately increase relevance, alignment and embeddedness of analytics to unlock ROI. With sound foundations, data manifests into competitive advantage.

Ensuring Relevant Metric Accessibility

The first dimension of analytics democratization involves granting widespread access to the right performance indicators fulfilling specific decision needs. Prioritize visibility into metrics balancing historic evaluation and predictive signals related to strategic goals, while de-prioritizing vanity or siloed metrics lacking clear actionability.

For example, spotlight leading indicators of deal risk like buyer budget trends, sales activity ratios and win/loss debriefs rather than retrospectively reporting lagging deal closure rates alone. Feature pump-priming metrics for pipeline health and foundational activities prominently over isolated output metrics.

This curation philosophy also enables constructive data dialogue across functions mitigating insular perspectives. Expanded diversity of inputs covering sales, marketing, finance and product views enriches context. Helping teams reconnect activities to overarching process and corporate goals also sustains focus amidst detail overload. Accessibility begets accountability.

Guiding Strategy Through Insights

Furthermore, inject forward-looking analytics directly into long-range strategic planning beyond short-term operations. Set the stage for this alignment by first identifying projected threats, market shifts or capability gaps possibly impacted 3-5 years out based on leadership wisdom. Then tap insights from macroeconomic projections, customer sentiment analyses, product adoption trends and other external and internal indicators to stress test assumptions and fine-tune scenarios. Run multi-variable simulations projecting performance under different strategies.

This foundation allows then guiding executives in long-term decisions on optimal sales resource allocation across regions and customer segments, pricing and discounting guardrails protecting margins, embedded partner ecosystems, and skilling investment priorities needed to win. Continuous feedback integrating real-world signals also helps further calibrate rollouts. With perspective, analytics progresses strategy.

Recognizing Patterns and Trends

Additionally, structure workflows eliciting emerging trends, anomalous outliers and sudden inflection triggers essential for alertness. Nurture pattern recognition across sales teams through structured mentoring on contextualizing numbers into insights. Look at performance spikes and dips through funnels. Review pacing trajectory changes in indicators week-over-week.

Help managers separate one-off variability from reproducible models needing intervention through root cause analysis and benchmarking normalized ranges. Have execs monitor markets for potential disruptive competitors and skunkworks teams evaluating internal innovations' scalability prospects. Create multi-lens hypotheses on deviations as learning opportunities, not just problems. Thoughtfully nurturing collective analytics acuity compounds capabilities over time.

Handling Uncertainty and Ambiguity

Today's business realities are growing more interconnected and fast-changing by the day. This inherent complexity means facing some degree of uncertainty or ambiguity in data - gaps between correlation and causation, limitations in predictive reliability over time, biases and assumptions baked into methodologies.

The instinct may be to oversimplify or avoid inconvenient uncertainties. But thoughtful transparency around analytics' fuzzy edges builds trust and safety for open curiosity instead of doubtful disengagement.

Promoting a Culture of Open Inquiry

The foundation for effectively handling uncertainty involves fostering an inquisitive culture encouraging exploration into analytical gray areas instead of penalizing knowledge limitations. Proactively structure constructive spaces for cross-functional teams to surface intellectual doubts, illuminate assumptions, and discuss constraints when reviewing ambiguous models, metrics or scenarios. Sustain collective interest before certainty by rewarding inquiry.

Leaders should drive this openness by clearly communicating reliability scores, confidence intervals, or probability bands intrinsic to the methodologies used - much like weather reports convey chances of precipitation. Highlight error bars, outlier exclusions, or gaps in input signals that naturally constrain wider applicability of any findings. Illuminate uncertainty contexts upfront through smart data storytelling.

Additionally, establish online discussion forums and working groups to thoroughly pressure test proposals dealing with uncertainty through techniques like hypothesis clarification, surrogate data testing, and other structured evaluative techniques borrowed from academic peer review. Diversify analytical scrutiny across different perspectives within and without the sales organization.

Communicating Complexity Visually

Also use interactive visuals to convey unavoidable ambiguity or uncertainty clearly. Well-designed data visualizations can map out multiple future scenarios - spanning potential market reactions, competitor responses, risks. This brings real-world dynamics to life visually over simplistic singular forecasts.

For example, show adoption rate predictions for innovations via branch charts. Convey not just the recommended path, but interactive slider bars that showcase key variables causing divergence based on different assumptions. Let users stress test assumptions through flexible, branching scenario models.

Regardless of uncertainty inherent in projections, maintain visual and navigational clarity so audiences focus on substance rather than form confusion. Prioritize simplicity over false precision when ambiguity exists. Present data stories showing multiple plausible outcomes, not absolutism. Enable people to transparently diagnose analytical limitations and tradeoffs. Remind them analytics cannot provide universal solutions, but rather enriches discussions through insight.

Thoughtful transparency around reliability gaps earns durable stakeholder trust even amidst disruption. While guaranteed perfection is impossible, data should inform strategies and spark insights if communicated with nuance. Lead visualizations with humility rather than overclaiming certainty. Embrace statistics to enlarge perspective, not restrict scenarios through facades.

Key Takeaways

- Guide teams to recognize causal chains and correlations between metrics instead of assessing KPIs in isolation. Synthesized data narratives reveal crucial performance drivers.

- Incorporate real-time visibility through automated dashboards and alerts tied to key metric thresholds. Enable rapid response to emerging issues.

- Facilitate open, non-judgmental data dialogues across teams to surface questions, knowledge gaps and assumptions that inform skill building.

- Ensure accessibility to leading indicators related to strategic goals while deprioritizing vanity metrics lacking actionability. Curate based on decision needs.

- Inject forward-looking insights directly into long-range planning scenarios and simulations to stress test strategy assumptions.

- Promote a culture encouraging curiosity to explore analytical uncertainties and limitations instead of avoidance or oversimplification.

- Lead visuals with humility when ambiguity exists. Convey reliability scores and confidence intervals to earn trust despite unpredictability.

Chapter 10

Applications of Data Stories in Sales Operations

D ata-driven storytelling brings statistics to life across essential sales operations responsibilities, bridging metrics to meaning for stakeholders through contextualized visual narratives. Strategic narratives make statistics accessible and memorable for diverse audiences, guiding leaders, marketers and sellers to aligned decisions through virtual experiences interacting with data-driven dashboards. Leveraging explanatory context, selective curation, visual encodings and exploration promoting transparency, analytics translations achieve widespread fluency elevating enterprise intelligence maturity.

When executed effectively, data stories illuminate performance gaps, showcase predictive insights, highlight decision tradeoffs and ultimately accelerate growth strategies.

Sales Performance Trend Analysis

Evaluating overall company revenue and sales growth using data narratives provides intuitive clarity for performance analysis otherwise lacking from scattered data points. Visualized narratives supported by key driver metrics over multi-year timeframes spotlight areas of strength, risks and opportunities to concentrate strategic priorities around.

Objectives:

- Quantify current sales scale and growth momentum

- Diagnose what factors influence performance results

- Guide executive planning and strategy targeting

Key Metrics:

- Total Sales Revenue - The total monetary amount generated from all products and services over selected periods, showing aggregate performance

- Sales Growth Rate - The percentage increase or decrease in total sales over comparable prior periods, indicating expansion or declines

- Conversion Rates - The percentage of prospects that become paying customers out of all leads engaged, signaling sales process effectiveness

- Customer Acquisition Costs - The total sales and marketing spending invested to convert each new customer, calculated by dividing total expenses by customers obtained, determining profitability feasibility

Context - Performance metrics quantify outcomes but require perspective. Sales should align to market conditions, economic cycles and competitive intensity shaping results. Executives need visibility into key statistical drivers tied to decisions within control such as targeting, product development and selling competency.

Analysis - Interactive sales dashboards contextualize market realities, providing navigable visual data stories to diagnose performance influencers. Granular analytics uncovers optimization opportunities across regions, customer segments, campaigns and product lines. Statistical driver interrelationships determine tactical priorities with highest growth impact potential if addressed.

Activation - Data-driven strategy alterations combined with tactical realignments in response to insights propels performance. Revised marketing targeting, expanded solutions for rising segments and improved seller skills training address identified gaps. Continual tracking ensures accountability to science-based enhancement initiatives guided by analytics revelations over time.

Customer Segmentation Analysis

Segmenting addressable customers based on common attributes, behaviors and value potential allows tailored journey matching through personalized strategies that lift relationship revenue.

Objectives:

- Recognize distinct customer clusters with differing underlying needs

- Inform targeting and tactical personalization to boost resonance

- Prioritize high-potential groups for resource focus

Key Metrics:

- Firmographics - Industry, specialty, years in business indicating interests and priorities

- Purchase history - Historical spend, product mix patterns signaling potential value

- Predictive Metrics - 2-year projected value, lifetime revenue estimates informing investment decisions

- Engagement Preference - Journey channel activity driving personalization

Context - Customer metrics remain aggregated statistics without linkage to identity and underlying priorities. Segmenting populations based on characteristics that shape motivations makes data actionably relevant.

Analysis - Interactive dashboards with filtering reveal variances across groups that guide unique value proposition tailoring and messaging for improved conversion outcomes based on known preferences. Heatmaps visualize expanding solution opportunities over time based on maturation indicators within projected lifetime timeframes across clustered subgroups.

Activation - Executing personalized promotions, partnerships and relationship managers matched to nurture paths for maximum mutual value based on intimately understood needs drives performance advancement. Testing response rates by segment informs ongoing optimization.

Sales Forecasting

Statistical predictive models empower reasonably estimating future period sales results based on patterns within historical data. Applying predictive analytics augments intuition with data for proactive planning.

Objectives:

- Establish insightful performance baseline forecasts

- Evaluate expansion opportunities and risk scenarios

- Promote alignment around data-driven growth projections

Key Metrics:

- Past Sales Trends - Trailing revenues over yearly quarters and peak seasons

- Conversion Rates - Closing percentages for active proposals and discussions

- Market Indicators - Macro factors like economic growth rates impacting buyer power

- Competitor Activity - Channel reports of new solutions swaying customer preference

Context - Historical sales patterns assume consistent external forces across data inputs for reliable applicability. Significant market shifts introduction uncertainty into baseline projections without re-calibration.

Analysis - Interactive forecasting dashboards leverage models to simulate performance scenarios based on historical trends and emerging factors applied statistically. Granularity down to the region, product line and customer segment predicts based on local variabilities and patterns.

Activation - Anchoring budgeting in data while welcoming scrutiny of modeling assumptions enables leadership dialogue. Updated projections as leading indicators change focus priorities amidst fluid landscapes. Promoting data fluency fosters continuous refinement.

Product Portfolio Analysis

Individually assessing internal product lines across dimensions like financials, customer value, competitive gaps and strategy alignment informs portfolio optimization decisions and innovation investments.

Objectives:

- Quantify current lineup performance distribution

- Diagnose risks from external solution advancements

- Spot unsustainable investments due to commoditization

Key Metrics:

- Sales Revenue - Product revenue, units sold and profit margin performance statistics

- Net Promoter Scores - External product rating benchmarks by features

- Customer Sentiment - Verbatim survey feedback on where value gained or lacking

- Competitive Benchmarks - Rating scores from analyst assessments of key features

Context - Pure financial returns alone overlook growing market spaces where competitive limitations suppress current customer acquisition. Declining revenue trends prompt evaluating external shifts necessitating realignment.

Analysis - Interactive product portfolio dashboards filtering dimensions like revenue, customer sentiment ratings and capabilities against alternatives inform views on individual and comparative performance to guide management decisions.

Activation - Scenario modeling tools allow visualizing portfolio optimization changes while assessing future innovations and capability growth opportunities through quantified narratives describing addressable gaps. Leadership deliberations benefit from contextualized data-driven dialogue around market dynamics usingPUSH analytics.

Sales Process Analysis

Evaluating conversion effectiveness through each process milestone from initial prospect awareness to becoming transaction customers reveals prioritized friction points for enhancement targeting to maximize yield rates.

Objectives:

- Quantify sales funnel fallout between process stages

- Diagnose obstacles undermining conversion performance

- Inform targeting, messaging and capability upgrades

Key Metrics:

- Lead Volume - Incoming prospect signal sources Indicates demand generation resonance

- Contact and Meeting Rates - Early access success securing conversations

- Proposal Acceptance - Solution resonance securing purchasing consideration

- Reasons for Losses - Direct diagnostics from lost deals analysis

Context - Conversion metrics demand contextualization like sales duration seasonality and asset engagement rates to interpret properly by comparing against historical precedent expectations given outside factors.

Analysis - Interactive sales funnel dashboard views map advancement rates through each milestone revealing prioritized friction points choking outcomes for future mitigation. Granular historical benchmarking provides calibration insights to evaluate severity.

Activation -Surfacing conversion obstacles promotes tactical response targeting through focused initiatives, whether enlarging qualifying inbound sources, enhancing consultative selling skills guiding consideration or launching market-informed solution updates closing competitive gaps.

Competitor Benchmarking

External sales competitor profiling compares capability maturity, solutions differentiation and position strength tracking threats while pursuing opportunities through channel leader engagement.

Objectives:

- Map provider landscape with growth levels

- Benchmark performance transparency

- Assess positioning and expansion options

Key Metrics:

- Market Size - Total addressable opportunity revenue

- Market Share - Percentage claimed against competition

- Competitor Ratings - External validated capability scores

- Marketing Reach - Followers and impressions signaling influence power

Context - Estimated total addressable market size sets revenue expansion expectations used for strategy prioritization planning. Changing market share percentages over time represent position strength trajectory signaling external strategy shifts necessitating preemptive response.

Analysis - Decision leader dashboards spotlight overall market room for growth visually overlaid with specific competitor penetration levels showing areas of leader entrenchment versus potential pockets of opportunity for expansion prioritization consideration prompted through supplementary gap identification analysis against internal assumptions.

Activation - Leverage competitive transparency diagnostics provoking product managers through comparisons against external innovation rates and marketing leaders based on audience engagement levels differences justifying best practice sharing arrangements across organizations to jointly lift market sophistication through nurturing focused channels benefiting all contributors constructively.

Sales Initiative Analysis

Marketing campaign and sales initiative investment analysis calculates return on investment (ROI) delivered based on tangible pipeline and revenue generation outcomes achieved compared to required resource expenditures supporting determination verdicts guiding continuity, recalibration or termination decisions as market conditions and asset viability shifts over time.

Objectives:

- Quantify campaign outcomes securing pipeline deals

- Weigh delivery costs against achieved returns

- Guide resourcing optimization and reallocation

Key Metrics:

- Pipeline Influenced - Total new opportunities added to forecast directly attributed to initiatives

- Cost Per Sales - Ratio of total budget invested divided by revenue wins credited

- Asset Performance - Tactics like emails sent, event attendance driving outcomes

Context - Pipeline and revenue return metrics connected to prior branded touchpoints measure campaign effectiveness strength converting audiences into quantified deal potential for gauging viable interest signal minimum thresholds justification relative to expenditures and labor calibration requirements.

Analysis - Marketing mix modeling tools statistically quantify multidimensional customer interaction influence capabilities empowering iterative ROI calculus scenario projections and variable dial turning for optimal configuration stress testing given constraints.

Activation - Embedded initiative performance tools automatically trigger ROI-justified rerun endorsements amidst calibrated market response signature updates or discontinuation warnings responsive to deterioration directly within command center dashboards to accelerate consensus gathering on optimal paths forward.

Sales Team Productivity Analysis

Seller pipeline progression and revenue outcome analytics tracks capability converting early stage prospect interactions into downstream closed deals measured against historical benchmarks and quotas informing coaching interventions towards improved collective results.

Objectives:

- Diagnose seller capabilities advancing opportunities

- Inform territory assignments and specialization optimization

- Boost critical competencies through personalized guidance

Key Metrics:

- Activity Volume - Calls, emails for messaging resonance

- Pipeline Sourced - Deals directly cultivated end-to-end

- Sales Cycle Velocity - Average progression pace from prospect to customer

- Revenue Influenced - Total contributions across all pipeline deals

Context - Granular sales activity metrics demand normalization across tenure, role specialization and territorial considerations for appropriate peer capability benchmarking given expected profile differentiations.

Analysis - Longitudinal pipeline dashboards overlay conversion fallout diagnosis revealing obstacles blocking optimal progression by individual resources for amelioration or realignment considerations prompted through supplementary performance insights report analysis by managers.

Activation - Automated sales coaching tools connect relative capability advancement opportunities to science-guided training recommendations showcasing incremental efficiency lift potential when addressing gaps.

Customer Journey Analysis

Customer journey mapping visualizes every touchpoint interaction that prospects experience across purchasing decision cycles. Pinpointing friction pain points inhibits conversion to prescribe improvements expanding market share through enhanced nurturing facilitation.

Objectives:

- Quantify existing market traction at each phase

- Diagnose decision fallout risks

- Boost supported consideration and selection

Key Metrics:

- Entry Sources - Initial channels introducing brand

- Research Behavior - Assets accessed across journey

- Sales Channel Engagement - Meeting types securing deals

- Exit Patterns - Detraction drivers from losses or churn

Context - Interaction frequency and depth by channel benchmarks relationship lifecycle progression trajectories setting expectations given current maturity constraints. Journey milestone prioritization occurs based on diagnosing patterns causing greatest customer detraction effect size warranting mitigation focus by leveraging contextual insights.

Analysis – Heat maps spotlighting cross-sectional fallout trends at different phases easily surface widespread hurdles for enhancement resource targeting by managers. Flow diagrams parsing populations by behavioral pathways into segmented groups provides a tailored sequence view matching observed precedence patterns.

Activation - Predictive analytics anticipating the likelihood of goals achievement amidst competing forces for individuals overlays journey steps to boost supported outcomes through automated triggers alerting on priority touchpoint servicing opportunities in real-time based on algorithmic assessments prescribed by data science insights.

Key Takeaways

- Spotlight sales performance trends over time using visualized data narratives enriched with contextual metrics that diagnose drivers to guide planning.

- Cluster customers by attributes and behaviors to inform personalized targeting and resource allocation matched to segment needs.

- Apply predictive models to reasonably estimate future sales results, weighing risks, based on patterns within historical data.

- Assess product lines across dimensions like financials and customer value to inform portfolio optimization and innovation targeting.

- Quantify sales process conversion fallout between funnel stages to diagnose obstacles and friction points for enhancement initiatives.

- Benchmark competitor positioning based on market share trends, ratings and growth to assess threats and expansion opportunities.

- Calculate marketing campaign ROI by quantifying pipeline and revenue directly attributed to initiatives against required costs.

Chapter 11
Conclusion

A s we wrap up our exploration of data-driven storytelling's immense potential, it merits underscoring how mastering contextual narrative techniques represents both an unparalleled opportunity and solemn responsibility for modern sales operations teams seeking to strategically guide their enterprises to new heights.

While acquiring ever-growing volumes of customer, performance and market data is easier than ever thanks to expanding channels and systems, deriving genuinely meaningful insights from metastasizing information chaos has arguably never been more crucial - or more challenging. Static reports overloaded with metrics lack resonance. High-level dashboards fail to change behaviors. Complexity obscures rather than illuminates.

Through deliberate cultivation of data-driven storytelling capabilities, sales operations leaders can transcend these pitfalls to help organizations navigate complexity, separate signal from noise and ultimately convert torrential data into intelligence that sticks to inform strategies. Specifically, investing in specialist storytelling capabilities and aligned analytics processes allows sales operations departments to continually craft simplified yet profoundly resonant narratives from vast inputs. These compelling accounts shine a spotlight that reveals crucial new market opportunities, validates proposed commercial plans with hard evidence and informs continual optimization of revenue motions based on quantitatively verified outcomes from past initiatives.

While traditional reporting focuses on simply collating historical indicators, data storytelling adopts an intellectually agile, opportunity-seeking mindset embracing the inherent complexity within statistics rather than avoiding inconvenient uncertainties. This empirically grounded philosophy challenges assumptions using facts, balances dialogue across perspectives and deliberately curates metrics to compel insight-driven convictions for change even amidst disrupted landscapes.

Informed storytelling thereby provides sales operations an avenue to gradually cultivate enterprise-wide fluency with data-based decisions organically over time. Instead of episodic dashboards passively consumed, embedding resonating narrative updates across processes, events and channels ushers quantitative intelligence into sales organization DNA - uplifting capabilities, uncovering blind spots and connecting insights into sustainable competitive advantage.

As customer behaviors, consultation-based selling models and virtual engagement technologies continue advancing rapidly, the need for continuous guidance through evidence-rooted stories only intensifies. Looking ahead, data-driven narratives will remain pivotal for strategically evolving sales representative competencies, sentiment-informed relationship strategies and predictive pipeline management tuned to unique market variabilities in order to maintain resonance.

The most forward-thinking sales leaders recognize rich opportunity behind liberating creativity from within growing analytics complexity through exploration of data's endless discovery pathways. Rather than defaulting to constricted reporting of superficial metrics without deeper meaning, insight-focused storytelling can reveal advantageous differentiators and future-proofing opportunities otherwise hidden. For any function seeking elevated strategic influence guiding commercial decisions, purposeful data narrative capabilities prove pivotal both in current market turbulence and navigating sales revenue's unpredictable frontier.